David J. Bilinsky

S0-DJM-171

# Amicus Attorney® in One Hour for Lawyers

Law Practice Management Section
American Bar Association

Cover design by Gail Patejunas.

Nothing contained in this book is to be considered as the rendering of legal advice for specific cases, and readers are responsible for obtaining such advice from their own legal counsel. This book and any forms and agreements herein are intended for educational and informational purposes only.

This publication was made possible with the generous financial support of Gavel & Gown Software, Inc., developer of Amicus Attorney® software.

Publication of this book should not imply endorsement by the American Bar Association or the Law Practice Management Section of the products or services of Gavel & Gown Software, Inc.

The products and services mentioned in this publication are under or may be under trademark or service mark protection. Product and service names and terms are used throughout only in an editorial fashion, to the benefit of the product manufacturer or service provider, with no intention of infringement. Use of a product or service name or term in this publication should not be regarded as affecting the validity of any trademark or service mark.

The Section of Law Practice Management, American Bar Association, offers an educational program for lawyers in practice. Books and other materials are published in furtherance of that program. Authors and editors of publications may express their own legal interpretations and opinions, which are not necessarily those of either the American Bar Association or the Section of Law Practice Management unless adopted pursuant to the By-laws of the Association. The opinions expressed do not reflect in any way a position of the Section or the American Bar Association.

© 2000 American Bar Association. All rights reserved.
Printed in the United States of America.

Library of Congress Catalog Card Number 00-132640
ISBN 1-57073-681-2

04 03 02 01 00     5 4 3 2 1

Discounts are available for books ordered in bulk. Special consideration is given to state bars, CLE programs, and other bar-related organizations. Inquire at Book Publishing, American Bar Association, 750 N. Lake Shore Drive, Chicago, Illinois 60611.

# Contents

## THE LESSONS

### LESSON 1

### LESSON 2

### LESSON 3

### LESSON 4

### LESSON 5

### EPILOGUE

## BEYOND THE LESSONS

# Acknowledgments

To Beverly Loder, Tim Johnson, and all the staff at ABA Book Publishing and the LPM Publishing Board who saw this book through to its completion and provided motivation and support; to Wendy Berry and Ron Collins and all the staff at Gavel & Gown Software, Inc., who equally supported this effort through their suggestions, corrections, and improvements; to Storm Evans (even Dan Coolidge!) and all other reviewers who generously gave their time and attention. Thanks to Gene Macchi for listening.

Thanks also to Jo-Anne and Lauren—Jo for creating the belief in the value of my work, and Lauren for providing the magic.

# Preamble

This book is intended for lawyers and legal assistants seeking a better way to manage their time, their files, their contacts and their communications. I have been using Amicus daily for years—and find it difficult to imagine life without it. This book is intended to help others gain a facility with and appreciation of how Amicus can change your life for the better. You could skip the *Introduction* as well as *Putting It All Together*—but I would not. It is difficult to give someone who doesn't have any history with a particular tool an insight on how it can improve the way they work. The *Introduction* and *Putting It All Together* are intended on showing you how you can effortlessly use Amicus to cross the river to the promised land. The other chapters provide the stepping stones. See you on the other side!

# Introduction

## Probing the Mists: A Day in the Life of an "Amicus" Attorney.

Think of a typical day in your office, and how often you reach for your desktop telephone index to obtain a telephone number, or refer to your printout of your active files to obtain a client address or file number or other relevant information about the file, or go to the filing cabinets to obtain the correspondence part of a file to get this information to dictate a letter, or refer to your handwritten To-Do list to make sure you haven't forgotten an important entry, or have your secretary come into your office to borrow your desktop calendar to make an appointment or check out a proposed trial date.

Sounds mundane? Perhaps. But consider the time saved if your electronic calendar is available across the network, and your secretary can call it up and make an entry for an appointment or a trial without disturbing you and without leaving her desk.

Also consider if a centralized list of all clients, addresses, fax numbers, telephone numbers (office, home, cell, and alternate) are maintained and kept up to date on the network. There would be no need to get a file to obtain a telephone number or to get an address for a letter or fax. Moreover, by a simple click of the mouse, you can create a fax cover sheet directly from the Contacts Manager and send it to the printer, with the correct name, address and fax number and confidentiality notice automatically inserted on the cover sheet.

Personal Information Managers (PIMs) can easily offer efficient and effective improvements to the way we organize our lives and in particular, carry on our practices. Amicus Attorney is legal-specific case manager or a practice management program which has many additional features not available in a generalized PIM. In this description of a day in the life of a lawyer, we have taken the features of Amicus Attorney to examine a typical "Day in the Life of an 'Amicus' Attorney."

## 8:30 AM

You arrive in the office and turn on your computer. After Windows fires up, you launch Amicus Attorney. First you examine your Daily Report, and scan to see the reminders of the appointments and deadlines you have scheduled for today. Then you enter the Calendar section of Amicus Attorney and examine your To-Do's. You run through your To-Do's, and look at the rankings of your items. While mentally going through your list, you recall something that you thought of yesterday evening and you create a new To-Do. After you assign your new entry a priority and link it to a file in your system, you reorder your list of To-Do's.

While in your Calendar you also review your scheduled appointments. Scanning for free time, you note that your most recent innovation, being a repeat appointment, from 8:30 to 8:40, has popped up on your calendar. This is an appointment that you have booked with yourself every morning at 8:30 to grab your cup of coffee, go through your appointments and schedule your day.

As you scan your telephone messages that were recorded by your voice-mail system last night, you schedule the time from 8:40 to 9:15 for returning these telephone calls plus those that you couldn't return from yesterday. Since your Amicus calendar is networked, your secretaries know that this time is meant for you to take calls but otherwise to be left undisturbed.

You also copy your five most important To-Do entries and drag and drop them into your calendar. This creates appointments in your day for these entries. Moreover, you grab the mouse and drag the start and finish time bars for these entries until you are satisfied with the times allotted to each one in your day. You set alarms to go off when there is ten minutes left in each allotted time slot, to allow you to determine at that point to schedule for more time for these tasks or to finish up what you have done to that point in time and go on to other things.

Having scheduled the five most important To-Do's in your day, you open your "Do Someday" list. This is your list of the items that, while not pressing and urgent, are VERY important, such as taking time to market your practice or to think about your long-term personal and career goals. You examine your schedule and schedule a 15-minute appointment to take time to "sharpen the saw," in the words of Stephen Covey.

## 8:40 AM

In the Amicus Call Center you create a "message slip" for each voice-mail message—knowing that the Amicus Call Center will now contain a list of all unreturned calls. You run across a voice-mail message where the telephone number is quite clear, but you can't make out the name of the person who called. You open up your Contacts Manager module and do a search on the telephone number. Immediately, a contact's name appears, together with a reference to a file in your system. On calling up the name of the file within the File Manager section of Amicus Attorney, you see that this contact is actually an expert that you have retained to prepare a report on your behalf. Having refreshed your memory, you use the dialer portion of Amicus Attorney to place the call and to start logging the call for time and billing purposes. During the call, you type in some notes. Upon the conclusion of the call, the notes are automatically logged in the phone call section of the file. You schedule a reminder to follow up on this matter in two weeks, to check if the expert has forwarded to you your requested report. Moreover, you dialog the printer icon to print up the summary of the telephone call for posting on your file (after all, you do still keep hard copy files SOMEWHERE in the office!).

Going through your other unreturned messages, Amicus logs each returned call and creates a time and billing entry within the Time Sheet module. Each message slip already contains the name of the file and the person you are calling back so creating a time entry is simply a few mouse clicks away and even the time expended is filled in. You take satisfaction in knowing that you are creating a neat and organized time record of your day as you go along—no trying to recall the files worked on and how much time was put in by you when you are trying to run out the door at the end of the day.

Some of the calls generate further To-Do's on their respective files. A "make this a To-Do" button assists you with this process. You click into the button, and create a new entry in your calendar. The To-Do entry is cross-linked to your files, and you can change the assigned priority and set both a start date and a deadline within your calendar module. As Amicus Attorney stores all of the background information already, creating the linkages takes no more than a few mouse clicks. One of the matters is a high-priority item but not due for some time, and you set a reminder date to go off in the future to ensure that it is attended to well before the deadline expires.

One of the calls is from a lawyer requesting an extension of time to file a response to your action. You call up the Bring Forward Reminder that was created to check if the other lawyer had replied in time, and extend the time by one month. Fortunately, since other trigger dates that are dependent on the filing of the response have all been cross-linked, changing the time for the filing of the response also automatically extends the trigger deadline reminders for those entries by one month. You know that if any new date falls on a weekend or holiday, Amicus Attorney will automatically schedule the reminder to the next business day, and so you do not need to worry that a date will be missed if it falls on a weekend. A few more mouse clicks and your time entry for this matter is entered into your Time Sheet as well.

## 9:15 AM

Your next recurring appointment reminder alarm goes off—to take ten minutes with your secretary and discuss what is happening today and what has to be done. Since the appointment is a group scheduled one, as well as a repeat one, her alarm has also gone off in her calendar and she appears at your door at the requisite time. You both sit down with your coffee and discuss what happened yesterday and what is in store today. She tells you of the requirement for her to prepare a list of documents on the Smith file that must be filed next week—which has popped up as a reminder to her on her calendar in Amicus Attorney.

You discuss with her the five priority items for you today. She reminds you that Ms. Jones will probably be calling sometimes today to discuss her matter, and you fire up her file within Amicus Attorney and type in a few brief notes on questions raised by your secretary and your proposed answers.

## 9:25 AM

You stretch, get up and go get more coffee prior to your first appointment—one scheduled with yourself at 9:30 to work on your first and most important To-Do that day. You type in your Amicus Calendar (which is shared on the office Network) that this appointment is "Code Red"—meaning that you don't wish to be disturbed and close your door. You click on the timer section of Amicus Attorney and click on this particular file entry and Amicus Attorney starts to log the time on which you are working on this file.

During this dedicated work time, you must call certain people regarding the file. You pull their numbers off the file found in the FILES module of Amicus Attorney. You log the calls and create memos of your conversations, which are done in the Phone Notes section, and they are automatically entered onto the file. You also click on the printer icon to create a hard copy of the memos of these conversations.

Also during this time you find that you must call people that do not appear in Amicus Attorney. You click "NEW" in the Contacts Manager module, and create a new entry for these people. Having then associated them with this file, you are confident that you never will need to search for their number again, and that they will pop up should you or anyone else in your office have need to locate them. Also, since you have made a brief entry in the File section of who these people are and why they are important to the file, anyone with appropriate security clearance could review the electronic file in Amicus Attorney and gain an appreciation of who everyone is associated with the file and how to contact them. You are comfortable knowing that an associate could pick up the ball on this file should something arise if you are out of town or ill.

## 10:20 AM

Your calendar alarm goes off telling you that you have ten minutes until your next scheduled appointment. You consider what you have accomplished and what still needs to be done, and you create a new To-Do to take the file the next step further. You create a note to the file within the Notes section of Amicus Attorney summarizing what you have done today, and print it up as a hard copy by simply clicking on the printer icon. You also close off the logger and use the time logged as a time entry for the file into the Amicus time sheet for the day.

## 10:30 AM

OK, time to return all the telephone calls that came in during your dedicated work time. You run through the voice mail and create "pink telephone slips" in Amicus's Call Center and add them to your list of unreturned messages in the Call Center. Starting with the least desirable call, in order to get it over and done with, you open the message slip and click the "phone" icon for Amicus to dial the person and start logging the call. You know that there will be follow-up things to do, and so you use the Notepad part of your New Phone Call Slip to jot down things arising during the call. After you hang up, you create two To-Do entries, and use the Contacts Manager to create a quick fax to confirm to the person called matters arising during your call and send it off to the printer (you considered faxing directly from your computer, but since you have a number of other calls to make, you would rather use the office fax to take care of that detail while you return those calls!). You finish off the time entry for this matter, and move onto the next telephone call.

The next call slip is from someone who isn't in your Contacts Manager. So you dial this one by hand, only to find out it is a new lawyer who has taken over an existing file. So as you are talking to her, you fire up your File Manager, and change the entry for name of the lawyer handling the matter to this new lawyer. You also use Amicus Attorney to send an office e-mail to your secretary and associates that the lawyer has changed. This way your secretary and everyone else who has need to reference this file will see the change of lawyer notation together with her address and fax number. You create a time entry, and go off to the next call.

You sigh as you see the next call slip. This is a lawyer with whom you have been playing telephone tag for days. It seems that he is intentionally unavailable every time you call. You consult your lawyers' directory, and see that he has an e-mail address. So you jump into your Contacts Manager in Amicus and enter his e-mail address into his contact information. From within Amicus Attorney you double-click on his email address—and a "new e-mail message" screen is automatically started, with the correct address inserted. You type in the rest of the e-mail message that summarizes the substance of your communication, and before sending it off, you ensure that you have clicked ON the option that confirms delivery of the e-mail, and send it on its way. You print up a hard copy for the file by clicking the printer icon, and then create a time entry for the file.

In this way you methodically go through your call slips, creating notes and To-Do's as you go, and logging the calls and creating time entries for your daily time sheet. One of the calls is from a potential new client. You obtain her name and the name of the opposing party with whom she is aggrieved, and quickly do a search on both names within the office-wide list of clients and opposing parties maintained in your networked Amicus Attorney. Confident that no one in the firm acts for the opposing party and confident that there are no apparent conflicts on this file, you continue with the call and make an appointment in your calendar for this new client to come in and meet with you. You create a new file in the Files section of Amicus Attorney, and type in the summary of your conversation into the Notes section for the file. You create a time entry for the daily time sheet, and move onto the next call slip.

## 10:55 AM

A voice starts singing out from your computer's speaker, and displayed on your screen from the Calendar portion of Amicus Attorney is a reminder that you have a conference call scheduled in five minutes. You click into the File Manager module and review the Notes that you have made for this file, and in particular, your objectives for this call. When the conference operator comes onto the line, you are up to speed and ready to roar.

## 11:10 AM

Your conference call completed, and your current telephone calls returned, you pop up your calendar to review the rest of the day and look over your To-Do's. You note that your next scheduled appointment is in ten minutes, which is an appointment booked with yourself to work on your second most-important To-Do today. You get up, stretch, and go for a short break and a coffee, pleased with your progress so far.

## 11:20 AM

On returning to your desk, you see that a reminder of your 11:20 appointment is on the screen. You type into your Amicus Calendar (which is shared on the office network) that this appointment is "Code Red"—everyone in the office can see that you are to be undisturbed. You start the timer logger on this file in Amicus Attorney and go at it.

## 11:33 AM

Your secretary pops her head into your office, and says although she knows you don't want to be disturbed, the lawyer to whom you had sent the e-mail this morning is on the line, insisting that he speak to you. You sigh, click on the Stop button on your timer, suspending the timer on the matter you were working on, and start it ticking away on this matter involving this irate lawyer. You take the call, and patiently listen while this particular bit of pomposity attempts to justify why he hasn't done what he has promised to do. In closing the call you agree on a new deadline for this lawyer, and jump into your calendar to adjust the To-Do date to receive this latest promised response. You know that your own reminder to yourself to produce a reply once you have received this communication from this lawyer will be automatically adjusted as well, since you have cross-linked the two future Bring Forward Reminders in Amicus Attorney. You click "stop" on the timer to create a time entry for your daily time sheet, and go back to your original file from which you were interrupted.

## 11:55 AM

Your computer speaks again. You check your reminder on the screen, and note that you are to have lunch with one of your partners to discuss some office matters. You close off the file on which you are working, click the "stop" button on the timer to complete the time entry in Amicus and head out the door.

## 1:15 PM

You arrive back from lunch, with a new screenful of telephone call "slips"in Amicus's Call Center and fire up your calendar to review your afternoon. Your next client appointment is in 15 minutes, and you have all these telephone calls to return. Moreover, your e-mail program reminds you that you have received new mail. Your telephone also starts to ring. Oh well, so much for Plan A you say as you take the call. Once into this call, you realize that this is a new priority item that must be taken care of today. You review your calendar, and decide that your fifth To-Do for which you set time aside in the afternoon must be bumped over to tomorrow. You drag and drop this appointment into tomorrow's schedule, and create a new appointment in its place to handle this latest crises. As you are doing this, your alarm goes off reminding you of your 1:30 appointment with a client. You create a time entry for your time sheet, and start the time logger to track your time during your client appointment. You get up to go meet the client in the reception area.

## 2:12 PM

You complete your appointment with this client, and note that you are running into the time that you set aside to work on a file. You click the "stop" button to complete a time entry for this last appointment, and take a minute for a breather. What should you do next? Work on the scheduled file, return your telephone calls or look at your e-mail? You decide to quickly scan your e-mail and in so doing, you fire up your e-mail program from within Amicus Attorney. Having received some mail relevant to an urgent file, you print up both the original copy for the file as well as your Reply, which was automatically sent off for delivery. You create time entries for reviewing your e-mail, and check the clock.

## 2:24 PM

After reviewing the telephone call slips in your Call Center, you decide that none of them are urgent and can wait while you finish off the task you scheduled for this time slot. You start Amicus's timer on this file, and dive in.

## 2:48 PM

You complete your task, and create a time entry for your daily time sheet. Your latest alarm has gone off and you see that your next appointment is in two minutes, and so you get up to take a walk and grab a coffee on the way to retrieve the client from the reception area.

## 3:00 PM

You start your timer to clock the time during this appointment. During the appointment, you use the Contacts Manager to compose a quick fax to one of the other lawyers on this file on matters arising during your appointment. You click the print icon in order that the fax can be sent by the office staff while you continue to deal with matters with your client.

## 3:25 PM

You close off the appointment, create a time entry for your time sheet and run through your telephone call slips in Amicus's Call Center. You return as many calls as possible prior to your Alarm going off for your 3:30 appointment to deal with that urgent matter that arose just after lunch.

## 3:30 PM

You start your time logger to track the time on this urgent matter. You turn on your Do Not Disturb button on your telephone, type in "Code Red" on your Amicus Calendar for this appointment with yourself, and off you go.

## 4:07 PM

Having completed this urgent task, and in so doing having created new To-Do entries in Amicus Attorney as well as future reminders for third parties to produce needed work, you review your Calendar. You have a choice. 4:00 PM was to have been your time to "Sharpen the Saw," in the words of Stephen Covey. You decide that this activity will take priority over your remaining tasks for the day, since it is a long range activity and you have been occupied with shorter range duties all day. You close your door, again put on the Do Not Disturb button on your telephone, and indicate through your Calendar that this appointment is "Code Red"—in this case, personal undisturbed time and take 15 minutes to concentrate on meeting your longer-range goals.

## 4:22 PM

Your 15 minutes is up, and so you clean up your desk and give yourself a "way to go" on having fit in your longer-range goals during such a chaotic day. Now to close off the day and start to prepare for tomorrow. You run through all your unreturned telephone call "slips" and launch your dialer and call logger as you return each one. Amicus Attorney records the time spent on each call for your daily time sheet.

## 4:50 PM

Since Amicus Attorney automatically removes all the call "slips" that were from people that you have been able to reach or leave a message for from your list of unreturned calls, you review the remainder of the calls and leave them for renewed attempts tomorrow. You look over your calendar for the day, and move appointment items over to tomorrow's calendar that didn't get completed today. Finally, you look at your To-Do list, and mentally review the items, and consider the priorities that you have assigned, since To-Do items left undone will automatically be on tomorrow's list. You also look at the monthly view of your calendar in Amicus Attorney, to get an idea of how your time is committed for the balance of the month. You jot down a few notes to yourself and adjust some of the To-Do's just as your 5:10 **alarm** goes off. You see that Amicus Attorney has reminded you that your daughter has a softball game tonight that you promised to go to watch and so you straighten up your desk, post your time entries for the day, and print up your time sheet in order that you have a hard copy of your time. Your last task is to schedule your computer to do a tape backup of your hard disk during the evening hours.

## 5:15 PM

You turn off the lights in your office and head out the door to your daughter's softball game with the knowledge that you made the best use of your time that day. You know that you have priorities to do tomorrow, and you are certain there will be more urgent and rush duties that are yet unforeseen, but you are comfortable that things will be taken in stride. You look forward to having a hot dog during the game!

# Orientation to Amicus Attorney

There are three different editions of Amicus Attorney, Version IV: Organizer, Advanced, and Client/Server. Although many of the features described in this book can be found in any of the editions and in some of the previous versions, this book was written specifically with the features of the Advanced and Client/Server editions, Version IV, in mind. Where applicable, I have mentioned features that pertain to a network version of Amicus.

Amicus Attorney works the way a lawyer does. The following is meant as an overview of the major components of Amicus Attorney and how they will be used. This is not intended as a "how to" use these features—this will come later. The purpose of this overview is to get you accustomed to the feel of Amicus Attorney and how it "looks" to you on your computer.

A note on the conventions used in this book. When you see a ▶ symbol, do the action requested. You will find an explanation in the paragraphs that follow that goes into further detail about what you are doing. For the rest of this chapter I have provided the directions if you wish to launch Amicus Attorney and see on your screen what is mentioned in this chapter's text. However, it is not necessary that you do this at this time for the purposes of this orientation. However, starting at **Setting the Stage** I will ask that you follow the suggested actions in order to see on your screen what I am demonstrating in the text.

*Advanced Tip: Items in Italics are not formally part of the lesson but are enrichment tips to extend your knowledge and use of Amicus Attorney. You may wish to come back to these after completing the book in order to take fuller advantage of the features of Amicus Attorney.*

▶ To start, launch Amicus Attorney.

As we progress through the book, you should see the windows and features mentioned in the book on your screen. This book is intended to be right next to your computer as we work through the features of Amicus Attorney and learn how to use them.

## Daily Report

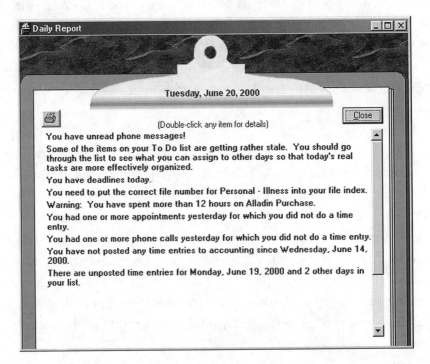

When you open Amicus Attorney for the first time in your day, you see your Daily Report. This report gives you a brief summary of the reminders from Amicus Attorney on your system. The Daily Report is your quick overview of your day. It serves as a nice reminder to clean up loose ends from your previous days (such as not making time entries for past appointments or telephone calls) and not posting your time to accounting. In one glance it tells you if you have any appointments or deadlines to attend to that day. By clicking on the Printer icon on the upper-left side of the "clipboard" you can create a printed copy of your Daily Report to remind you to jump to these issues first thing or work them into your daily schedule. We will deal with the Daily Report later in the book.

▶ For the moment, click "Close."

## Office

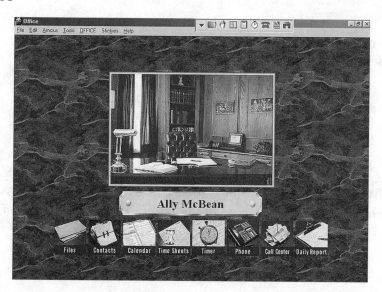

You should see your Office with a picture of a lawyer's desk (which can be personalized), and a number of icons with names such as "Files,"

"Calendar," "Contacts," "Time Sheets," "Timer," "Phone," "Call Center," and "Daily Report." These icons serve as jumping-off points to the different components or modules of Amicus Attorney. By clicking on each of these icons, you can enter the different components of Amicus Attorney.

Notice also that there are pull-down menus on the top left of the Amicus Office window with names such as: "File," "Edit," "Amicus," "Tools," "OFFICE," "Stickies," and "Help." These menus help you set up and configure Amicus Attorney to work they way you want it.

*Advanced Tip: Once you have completed this book, I highly recommend that you spend some time exploring the preference settings that can be found on the "File" drop-down menu. This will extend your ability to customize Amicus to work as you wish.*

The icons on your desktop are also represented in a Toolbar that can remain "on top" of any applications that you have open.

This toolbar will provide a quick method of entering Amicus Attorney from whatever else you may be doing on your computer, even when running other programs. To gain maximum use of Amicus, I recommend that you start Amicus Attorney first thing in the morning and keep the toolbar on top of all applications during the day. We will find out how to do this later in the book.

▶ Click on the Files icon. You will see:

## The File Manager

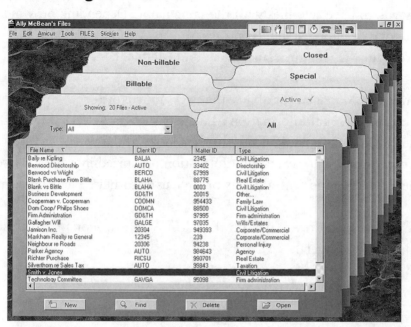

This component works like an electronic version of your paper files. You open a new file and assign to this file a Short File Name, Client Name, Matter Name, Client ID, Matter ID, Billing Status, Billing Rate, and File Summary. The File Summary is a note that can be a short synopsis of the file or of its particular relevance to you. Once opened, the file is part of your Amicus Attorney system and can be used and referenced in the other components of Amicus Attorney. Furthermore, if you integrate Amicus with your computerized accounting package, you will be able to take advantage of the integration features—such as directly posting your time to the accounting package, as well as having to open files only once for use in both Amicus and your accounting system.

Akin to your paper system, to avoid problems, you would not normally have two files with the same identification number or code. To assist in this, Amicus Attorney keeps track of your Short File Name and will not allow you to have two files with the same name. Depending on which accounting or billing system you use, Amicus Attorney will also help guard against having the same Client and Matter ID's as well.

It is this File Management ability that sets Amicus Attorney apart from generalized Personal Information Managers such as Act!, or Maximizer, Organizer, or Outlook. Amicus Attorney looks at the world through the eyes of a lawyer who wants all information organized in a file for later reference. Hence the central focus of Amicus Attorney's File Manager.

▶ Close this window (Click on the Close Window icon ☒ to close the File Manager).

▶ Click on the Calendar icon. You will see:

## The Calendar Manager

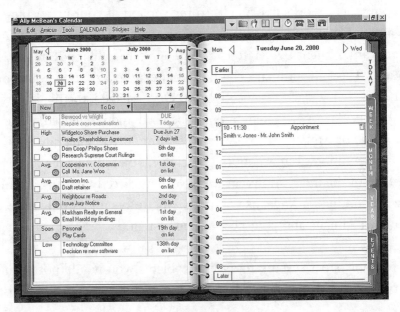

The Calendar module works like a paper Day-Timer®—but on steroids! The added features of an electronic calendar will quickly assert themselves (and become essential to how you work!). You can easily enter appointments, and when the times change, simply drag and drop the appointment to the new time. Note that your To-Do's are displayed on the left side of the page. These "To-Do's" have the advantage of automatically being carried forward until marked "done." By clicking on the tabs, you can quickly view your calendar in a weekly, monthly, or yearly format.

▶ Click on any date in the small month-at-a-glance calendars on the top left of the screen and you will jump to that day.

▶ Go back to "Today" by clicking on the Today tab.

In the Lessons we will explore how to schedule appointments, change appointments, and create repeating appointments (such as yearly reminders to create annual reports or annual reminders of your partner's birthday).

▶ Click on the ⊠ to close the Calendar Manager.

▶ Click on the Contacts icon. You will see:

## The Contacts Manager

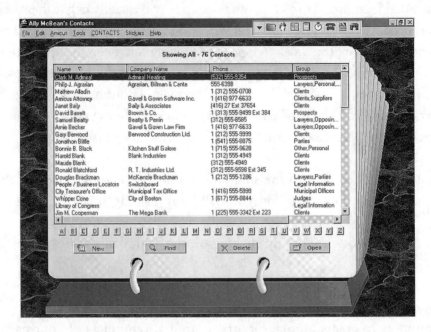

The Contacts Manager serves as your electronic Rolodex®. Here you can enter all contact information on lawyers, clients, consultants, and all other people with whom you have reason to reach—whether it be by mail, email, fax, or various phone numbers. One of the benefits of Amicus is the ability to associate persons in your Contacts Manager with your Amicus Files, Appointments, To-Do's, etc. If you have entered someone into the Contacts Manager in Amicus, and their address, telephone number, or other contact information changes, then that change will be reflected on every File, Appointment, and To-Do—anywhere this person is referenced in Amicus.

You can perform conflicts checks using this module quickly and easily. You can sort your contacts by company, by name, by group, and by contact date (useful for keeping in touch with clients). Your Contacts Manager can be configured to remind you to call a client on a predetermined schedule (that you determine).

▶ Click on the ☒ at the top-right corner to close the Contacts Manager.

▶ Click on the Timer icon. You will see:

## Timer

The Timer serves as your "Logger" to track your time on your files. Open a file from your list and your timer starts to log the time on the file. Telephone call? Click on the file regarding the call and the Logger will record the time on the call. Click "Stop" and go back to the original file. In this way, you can track all the time on all the files that you work on, effortlessly.

▶ Click on the ☒ at the top-right corner to close the Timer.

▶ Click on the Time Sheets icon. You will see:

## Time Sheets

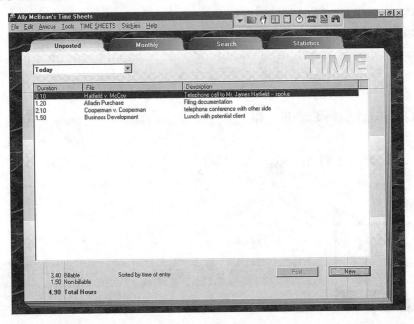

The Time Sheet is one great feature of Amicus Attorney. As you work your way through your day, you can create your time entries as you go. Many times Amicus Attorney will create and complete the time entry for you. Amicus Attorney will also total them as you go and show you how you have spent your day. Forgot to make an entry? No problem. The Daily Report will remind you that you forgot to make any entries on business days that are "blank." Or, simply click on "New" and select the file that you worked on, enter the date and time and—bingo!—your daily time is updated. The Time Sheet improves on your paper Day-Timer® as it totals your time as you go along. This feature is not found in any of Amicus's major competitors and is a major plus.

▶ Click on the ⊠ at the top right corner to close the Time Sheet.

▶ Click on the Call Center icon. You will see:

## Call Center

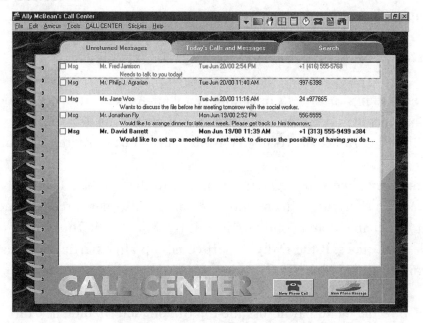

The Call Center is an excellent way to track all your telephone messages and phone calls. It tracks messages taken by others (your secretary, for instance, if you are networked), and displays them on your computer—automatically. The Call Center is a handy way to use Amicus to record, track, log, and time all your voice messages. Creating a "message slip" for each call allows you to centralize all your calls in one list of unreturned messages. It also allows you to manage those calls by either returning the call, creating a To-Do item for another day or, my favorite, by forwarding it to someone else (the most important time management tool—delegation!).

▶ Click on the ☒ at the top right corner to close the Call Center.

So now you have had a brief introduction into the main components of Amicus Attorney. Before we go to **Lesson 1: The File Manager,** and start working with Amicus Attorney, we need to make sure you have completed a couple of set up items.

## Setting the Stage

▶ First things first—let's open and run your Amicus Attorney by double-clicking on the Amicus Attorney icon on your desktop, or by choosing Amicus Attorney IV from your "Start" program menu.

I would now like you to get acquainted with the Toolbar. The toolbar serves as a shortcut to the features of Amicus Attorney. I recommend that you enable it and configure it so it is "Always On Top," and accessible at all times. If the Daily Report comes up after starting Amicus Attorney, click "Close."

▶ Go to the menu bar across the top of your screen and click on "Amicus."

▶ Then click on "Office Toolbar."

You should see either the large or the small toolbar:

Whether you use the small or the larger version is personal preference. You can change the toolbar's shape and size by clicking on the "▼" symbol on the left side of the toolbar.

▶ From the ▼ pull-down menu, select "Always On Top."

In this way, your Toolbar will always be accessible from any application that you have running. By left-clicking on the toolbar and holding, you can drag the toolbar and position it on your desktop wherever you prefer. Personally speaking, I like my toolbar to be at the upper-right of my screen near the "minimize" and "close" buttons.

There are several other ways to navigate within Amicus Attorney, including keyboard shortcuts for those of you who prefer to use them. For those of you who prefer "right click" navigation options, Amicus Attorney offers that feature as well.

*Advanced Tip: You will also notice a small* ❶ *icon on many of the windows in Amicus (for example, the Event, Phone Call, or Message windows). This is the info button and it allows you to automatically open the file or contact card currently being referenced from within that activity. This feature is very handy, especially when you have a client on the phone and you need further information—fast!*

Throughout this book we are going to use the Toolbar or the buttons on the Office window to navigate within Amicus. I promise to tell you how to navigate by giving you instructions which are indicated by the ▶ symbol.

To start using Amicus Attorney, it first must learn a little about you in order to properly open files and execute various functions.

▶ So to start from the "OFFICE" window in Amicus, click on "File" to display a drop-down menu in the upper-left corner of your screen.

▶ Then click on "Setup."

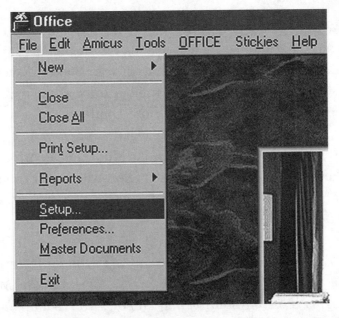

The following window will display:

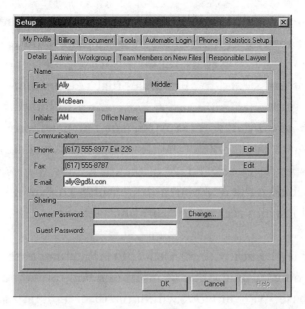

▶ Fill in the information (as necessary) in the tabs described below,
then click OK when done. I have noted below which information is
optional for performing the lessons in this book.

▶ *Details:* This tab contains your name, phone and fax numbers, email
address, and passwords to your Amicus Office. (Complete this, please!)

▶ *Admin:* This tab displays information entered by your team administrator, such as your User ID, whether you are a timekeeper, your
group memberships, and your accounting link. Any required
changes to the information in this tab must be made by your team
administrator. (Optional)

▶ *Workgroup:* You can specify a set of team members and/or team
member groups that you wish to display as a default each time the
Select Team Member dialog box is shown to you in Amicus Attorney
(for example, when scheduling an appointment). (Optional)

▶ *Team Members on New Files:* Each time you create a new file, it will be assigned by default to the team members you select in this tab. (Optional—but very useful for ensuring your associate lawyer or assistant is assigned to all the files that you open.)

▶ *Responsible Lawyer:* You may designate one particular timekeeper to be assigned by default as the Responsible Lawyer—the lawyer who is responsible for carriage of the file—on new files you create. You may change the designated Responsible Lawyer directly on individual files if necessary. (Please complete!)

Amicus Attorney comes with an installed tutorial database. For the purposes of going through the lessons in this book, I would like you to use this database. We will work within the tutorial database as we progress through this book.

▶ So, to open the tutorial database from the Amicus Office, click on "OFFICE" to enable the drop-down menu, and from this menu, click on "Open Tutorial Office":

A dialog box will then open.

▶ From within the options displayed in the dialog box, click on "Tutorial with full sample data" and then click on "Open."

This will launch Amicus' sample tutorial database and allow us to work in this database without affecting your own personal database. When you wish to exit from the Tutorial Office, go to the Amicus Office, click on "OFFICE" to enable a drop down menu on the top of your screen and then click on "BACK TO MY OFFICE." Closing the tutorial office resets the information so it is always current. Any changes you have made will not be saved. This allows you to experiment with the information in the tutorials without losing the integrity of the instructions.

▶ When you open the Tutorial Office, the Daily Report will appear. We won't need this for our lessons so click on "Close" and we will be taken to the Tutorial Office.

# The File Manager— Opening New Files, Working with Files

## Overview

So this is where the rubber meets the road. The major advantage of Amicus Attorney over generalized personal information managers is that Amicus is organized around an electronic file structure. This file structure mirrors the way that files are organized in your office, with file numbers, matter ID's, and short file names. However, it goes much further, as Amicus Attorney also records billing status (Billable, various Non-Billable designations, Vacation, and Personal), as well as the billing rate to apply to this file (Contingency, Discount, Normal, Premium, Flat-rate, Non-Billable, and Other). You can also set up the file to use UTBMS (Uniformed Task-Based Management System) codes should any of your clients require them. You can divide your files into lists of Active, Special, and Closed files. You can choose from an extensive list of file types (Litigation-Plaintiff, Wills & Estates, Real Estate, and Securities, for example). The list of file types is user definable, meaning you can edit or add to them to suit your practice requirements. In addition, you can set up 50 custom fields per file type. Although a file in Amicus Attorney already holds a lot of information, the custom fields allow you to track details that may be unique. The information can be used when creating documents or reports (customization is done in the Administration module of

Amicus Attorney—not the user modules that we are referencing here). Furthermore, you can build in alarms if you haven't made a time-entry on a file for a specified number of days or if your time on a file exceeds a specified limit. This means that you have an automatic bring-forward (BF) system as well as a monitor to prevent the billing on a file from getting out of hand.

Now to the File Manager. You can access the File Manager several ways.

▶ The two most common methods are by clicking on the Files icon from either of the following:

The Amicus Office desktop:

The Amicus Toolbars:

Each will take you to the File Manager, which looks like:

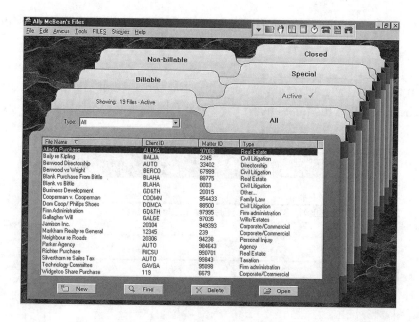

The objective of this lesson is to teach you how to open a file, add people to a file, and log a phone call from a file.

First let's open a file. Notice the buttons across the bottom of your files index:

▶ Click on "New." This will launch the open file dialog in Amicus.

You should see:

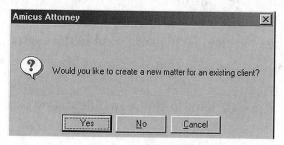

Clicking on "Yes" is one Amicus's shortcuts for creating multiple files for the same client.

▶ In this case, we are going to create a file for a totally new client, so we click "No." This takes us to the New File dialog screen, as follows:

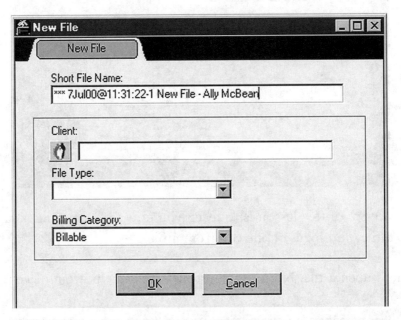

This New File opening screen prompts you to enter the essential information to open a new file.

▶ Type a short file name, for example Smith v. Jones, and press the "tab" key or move your mouse to go to the next field.

The label on the next field is "Client," and it also contains a "people" icon—which is the same icon that is on your Toolbar.

▶ Click on the people icon in the New File dialog box. You should see:

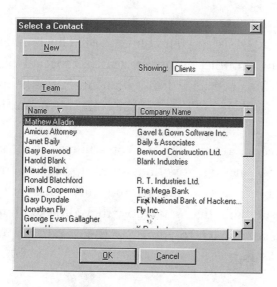

If you were opening a file for an existing client, you could select the client from the displayed list of clients.

▶ However, in this case we are creating a file for a new client, so we click on "New." You should see the following screen:

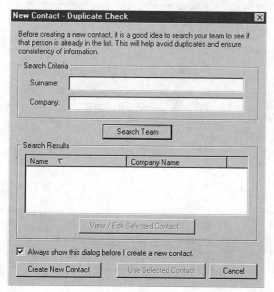

When adding a new contact, Amicus Attorney will prompt you to search to see if they already exist in your contacts list. This is an excellent opportunity to do a conflict of interest search, especially if you are using Amicus Attorney in a networked environment. Enter the individual's surname (or first few characters) and the company name, if applicable.

▶ Click the "Search Team" button. You will receive a "Sorry, no matches found" message if nothing turns up in the Contacts Manager. If a match is found, then the "hit" (or hits as the case may be) will be listed in a dialog window that allows you to verify if they are indeed a match to your search. For our purposes, let's say no match is found.

▶ Now, click the "Create New Contact" button. You should see:

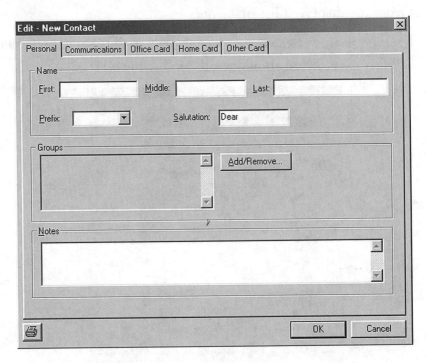

This screen allows you to enter contact information on the person to whom the file will be billed. You can use the tab key or, alternatively, the mouse, to move around.

▶ Enter "John" and "Smith" for the first and last names. Choose a prefix (Mr., Ms., Mrs., etc) from the list and enter a salutation if you want (if no salutation is entered, Amicus Attorney will automatically use the prefix and the last name on any correspondence).

▶ Next, we need to tell Amicus who this person is by specifying to which contact group or groups the individual belongs. Click the "Add/Remove" button, then:

▶ Click on "Clients" from the list and click "OK." This tells Amicus that John Jones is a client. We will cover more on groups in the next chapter—this is sufficient for now.

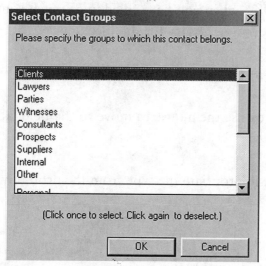

▶ Now, click on "Office Card" to enter the office address for John Smith, your new client.

Notice that there are multiple tabs for contact information. Clicking on the Home Card tab allows you to enter home information. Notice that you can enter multiple phone, fax, and other telephone numbers under the home address or on the "Communications" tab. You can also enter an email address.

▶ For future purposes, enter "jsmith@hotmail.com" in the email address section. You can come back and edit this contact information at any time.

▶ For future purposes in this lesson, please at least enter a phone number and office address. Notice that at the bottom left of each address card is an option to tell Amicus which address is the "primary" address. For our purposes, make the "Home" address the primary one.

▶ Click on "OK" when you have filled in as much contact information as you deem necessary for the file.

You will return to the New File opening dialog screen.

▶ Press "tab" or use the mouse to move to the field labeled "File Type."

▶ Click on the appropriate file type from the drop-down list.

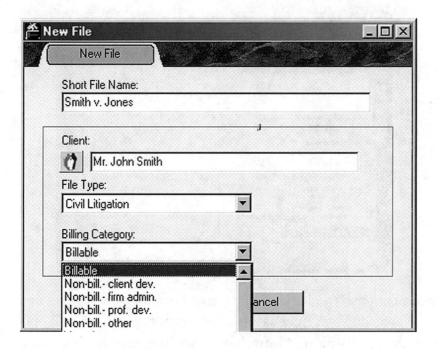

The next field, "Billing Category," will automatically default to "bill-able" unless you have changed your Preferences.

▶ You can click on the drop-down list to change the setting for a par-ticular file.

▶ When completed, click on "OK" to close down the dialog boxes.

VOILA!! You have done it! Amicus will now display the new Smith v. Jones file:

Congratulations! You have just mastered both the new file and new contact procedures in Amicus Attorney. From here on, we will build on the Smith v. Jones file and learn how to use the other tools in Amicus Attorney. The essentials are very similar and you will find that Amicus Attorney operates in a very similar manner in the other modules. Furthermore, you can see that Amicus Attorney is very graphical and intuitive, and due to its dialog screens, very helpful in guiding you through use of the program.

Moving around the screen, you can see that Amicus will collect optional file and client information.

▶ You can indicate if your client is an individual or a corporation by clicking on the appropriate circle.

A file in Amicus Attorney not only lists the names of the individuals involved, it also accumulates a wealth of information from the other modules.

▶ While we are in the File Manager, let's look at some of the other details. Near the top right-hand side of the page, notice a down triangle—click on it and you will see the following:

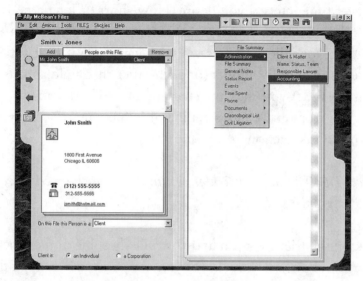

Notice that you reveal a drop-down list of other information that Amicus Attorney can and will keep on your client's file.

Each item on this drop-down menu contains additional information about this file. Under "Accounting" you can set up information such as the names of others in your firm who may work on the file or the Client and Matter IDs required by your accounting system.

▶ For example, click on the Accounting option and then "Responsible Lawyer." You will see that you have been added as the "Responsible" lawyer on this file. This can be changed, if required, at any time.

You will also see under the "Warn Responsible Lawyer if" section some of the case management abilities of Amicus Attorney. I suggest in most cases that you leave the "bring forward/reminder ability" checked—this will enable Amicus's automatic file tickler system. Notice that you can change the reminder period from the default ninety days to whatever time interval you desire. How short or long a period you choose is dependent on your practice and how often you wish to be prompted on your files. Amicus will also warn you if your total billable time exceeds twenty-five hours (or such other threshold as you determine) on the file if you click the enabling box. This setting in Amicus prevents you from exceeding a ceiling of billable hours on any file and allows you to take action as a result.

*Advanced Tip: The default tickler settings can be changed or removed in your Preference settings.*

▶ Click on the triangle again and you will see some of the other items that Amicus Attorney tracks for you. As you work through the system and do time entries, make phone calls or schedule events such as appointments or tasks for this file, the items will be automatically cross-referenced to this file. In a network environment, you can see the activities of others on this file. As we work through the rest of the lessons, you can go back to this file to view and see how this is done.

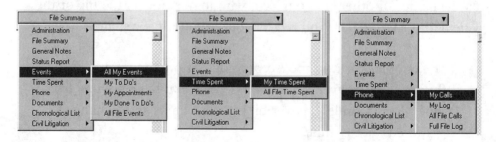

Congratulations! Now, onwards to **Lesson 2: The Contacts Manager.**

# The Contacts Manager —Adding People to Files and Events

In this lesson you will learn how Amicus Attorney allows you to keep track of all the people who are relevant to the Smith v. Jones file, and how Amicus Attorney organizes contacts around its file structure feature.

If you are still viewing the Smith v. Jones file, we will continue to use this file. If you have exited from the Tutorial Office, the Smith v. Jones file will no longer be in your Files index. As the Tutorial Office does not save changes (to preserve the integrity of the data), you will have to reopen the Smith v. Jones file or use the Hatfield v. McCoy file (which is part of the tutorial database), in which case our client will be John Hatfield. Substitute these names in the following instructions as appropriate.

If you need a refresher, the beginning of Lesson 2 explains how to start Amicus Attorney and open the sample tutorial database.

▶ From the Office screen or from the toolbar, click on the Files icon:

You should see the list of active files in your database, including the Smith v. Jones file:

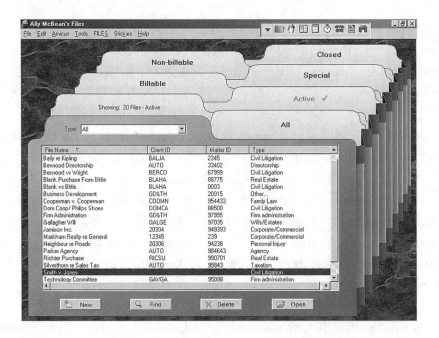

▶ Double-click on the Smith v. Jones file to open it (or alternatively, click once on Smith v. Jones and then click on "Open" or press the

enter key. The double-click feature is a short-cut in Amicus
Attorney). You should see the following:

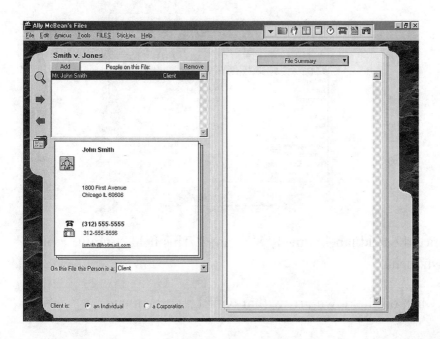

Look at the area "People on this File." Notice that there are two buttons "Add" and "Remove." These buttons are used to populate the file
with those individuals and corporations who are relevant to the file.

Let's start by adding in the name of the lawyer for Paul Jones (or
Frank McCoy), the Defendant.

▶ Click on "Add." You should see:

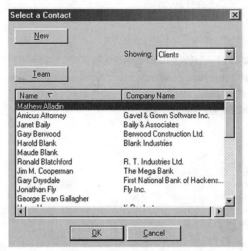

Notice the field label named "Showing." This field contains a pull-down menu.

▶ Click on the down arrow that will access the menu.

▶ Then click on "Lawyers."

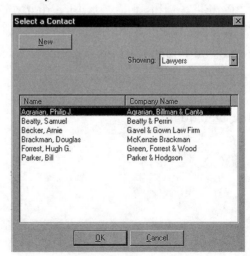

We are looking at the lawyers whose names have already been entered into the Amicus database. Notice Samuel Beatty of Beatty & Perrin.

▶ Double-click on this lawyer (or alternatively, click once on Samuel Beatty and then click on "OK." Remember that the double-click in Amicus is a shortcut).

You should see the following:

Bingo! Samuel has been added to the Smith v. Jones files. However, there is still a little to be done. Notice the wording that states: "On this File this person is a:", next to which is accesses another pull-down menu.

▶ Click on the down-arrow to activate the menu. You should see:

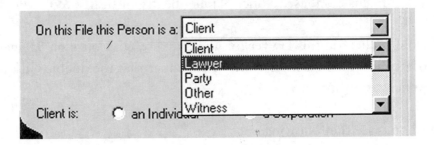

Notice the vertical scroll bar that moves you through the menu list.

▶ Scroll until you see "Lawyer" and then click on it. You should see:

Aha! We are starting to probe the depths of Amicus Attorney. Notice that the Contacts icon (same as the one that appears on the toolbar) has appeared.

▶ Now, when we click on this Contacts icon, we can enter the contact information for Paul Jones, the Defendant. Notice that our contact database will contain the name of the defendant (or defendants, if there are several of them), their lawyers, and contact information. Having a complete list of lawyers and all parties on all files will enable you to do quick conflict of interest checks on your desktop (as we did in the previous chapter).

*Advanced Tip: Amicus Attorney will act as your conflict checker—and will do so for the office provided that you are using Amicus Attorney across the network and all lawyers have entered all their files and parties into Amicus Attorney.*

Moreover, as we will see, we can also enter all consultants, physicians, experts—indeed anyone who has any bearing on a file—into Amicus Attorney (if you wish, contact "groups" can be defined by the user). In this way, you can quickly search the database and determine if any lawyer, party, expert, etc. is involved in any other files anywhere in the office.

▶ Lets go ahead and click on the Contacts icon next to "representing." You should see:

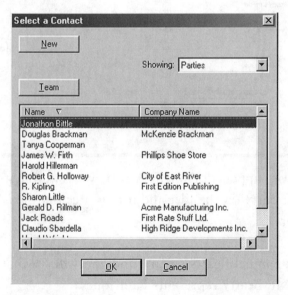

Notice that you are taken to the list of contacts—but that they have been filtered to display "Parties." Type the first few letters of "Jones" (or "Hatfield").

▶ If Paul Jones doesn't exist in our contact database, click on "New" and enter in Paul Jones with as much address and contact information as you wish (to facilitate this exercise, we have already entered him in the database).

▶ When you are finished, hit "OK" and you should see:

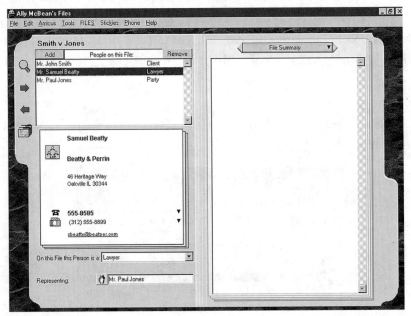

Two things have happened: Amicus Attorney has automatically added Paul Jones as a party on the file, and it indicates that he is represented by Samuel Beatty.

▶ "Click" on Samuel Beatty's name and you will see that Amicus indicates that Mr. Beatty represents Paul Jones.

Similarly, you could enter in the name of the surveyor who verified that Paul Jones trespassed onto John Smith's land, the name of the Judge (if one was assigned to the court file), the arborist who valued the trees cut down from John Smith's land, and the name of the tree-cutting firm that was hired and directed by Paul Jones to clear the trees from the Jones land (and is alleged to have done so on the Smith lands).

*Advanced Tip: I would like to draw your attention to a couple of things. First, although you are in the Files module of Amicus Attorney, adding a person to a file automatically adds them to your full Contacts list. Furthermore, when you view your full Contacts list, everyone in your file will appear.*

There are several ways to access your contacts.

▶ You can click on the Contacts icon in your toolbar,

▶ or, if in a file, double-click on one of the "People on this File" to be taken directly to their contact card.

▶ For now, click on the Contact icon on your toolbar.

This should take you to the index in the Contacts Manager module (if not, click on the Index button). By scrolling down your list of contacts, you should see "Paul Jones" or "Jones, Paul" (it is a user preference to display first name first or last name first, although names are searched by last name either way) and that he is grouped under "Parties." Similarly, his lawyer Mr. Beatty would also appear shown under "Lawyers."

Scroll down to Samuel Beatty's name.

▶ Double-Click to open his contact card (or alternatively, click once on Samuel Beatty and then click on "Open" or press the enter key). You should see the following:

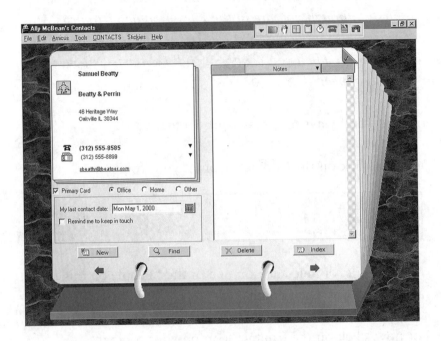

There is one other feature I would like you to see. On the bottom left of his contact card, you will see an area that states: "Remind me to keep in touch," and a box. Amicus Attorney will prompt you to contact your client on a predetermined schedule (great for keeping in touch with your clients and keeping up on your files). The default is ninety days—but you can select whatever period is comfortable for you. I know some lawyers who contact their clients every thirty days—this is a great way to automatically prompt for this without using any other systems or staff time.

*Advanced Tip: Use the "Remind me to keep in touch" feature to gener-ate reminders to yourself to contact your clients on a regular schedule. Clients love to have their lawyers call them to catch up on news rather than always having to call their lawyers. Earn brownie points!*

On the right-hand page of the contact card you will see the following:

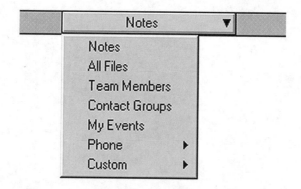

*Advanced Tip: Click on the triangle to reveal a drop-down list of other information that Amicus Attorney is tracking for this contact. Click on "All Files" to see the files that are associated with this person as well as their role on those files. Clicking on "Team Members" will show you the people in your firm dealing with this individual. Clicking on "Contact Groups" will display and edit the groups to which this per-son belongs. Furthermore, clicking on "My Events" and "Phone" will display any appointment, To-Do item, or a log of all calls and mes-sages with this person. Lastly, clicking on "Custom" will display any or all of the twenty custom fields you can set up for your contacts.*

You can see how Amicus Attorney uses the Files Manager and the Contacts Manager to work together to organize and place your con-tacts into the file structure of Amicus. As a result, you create a compre-hensive database that can be used for conflicts checks. You can also use Amicus to keep you on top of your files and your clients by automatically prompting you to review your files and contact your clients on a schedule that is suitable to you and your practice.

Well Done! In the next lesson, we will use the Calendar Module of Amicus to create To-Do lists for your files.

# The Calendar
# —Appointments,
# To-Do's, and Events

In this chapter we are going to make appointments, To-Do's, and create events on your files. We will see how the file structure of Amicus simplifies the process of working with your files and your calendar—all from your desktop.

First, let's open the Calendar module.

▶ From the Office screen or from the toolbar, click on the Calendar icon:

You should see:

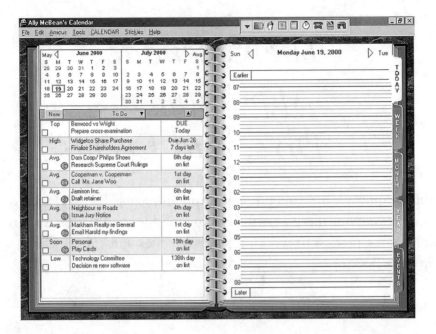

Take a few moments and familiarize yourself with this module. At first glance it appears to be a standard business appointment layout—two months-at-a-glance on the top left, the current day with times for appointments on the right, and a To-Do list on the bottom left. However, there is much more here than immediately meets the eye. Time to start going.

First off, let's create an appointment. Let's say that you have arranged to meet with your client at 10:00 AM today to talk about his file. It is expected to be a lengthy meeting and as a result, you have set aside 1.5 hours for the meeting. So how do we create this appointment?

▶ First, point your mouse at the 10:00 AM line in the appointment part of the screen. Hold down the left mouse button while you drag the mouse down to 11:30 AM and then release the mouse. What happened?

A new appointment/event dialog box should have opened, which looks like this:

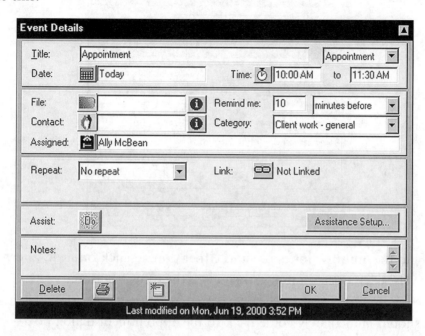

Notice that an appointment at 10:00 AM today has been created, lasting 1.5 hours to 11:30 AM. Let's add some information to this appointment.

▶ First click on the File icon that is part of the dialog:

You should be presented with a list of active files that looks like:

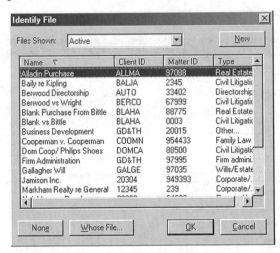

▶ Find the Smith v. Jones file and either double-click on it or, alternatively, click once on it and then click the "OK" button.

You should immediately come back to the appointment dialog box—notice that Smith v. Jones has been inserted into the "File" area. You should see:

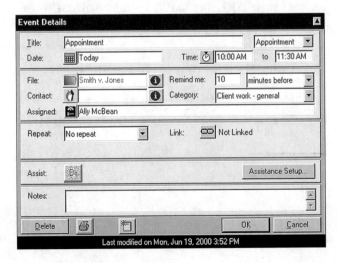

▶ Next, click on the Contact icon that looks like:

Notice that you are taken to the Contacts list for the Smith v. Jones file. The people that we have associated with the Smith v. Jones file should appear in a list, which looks like:

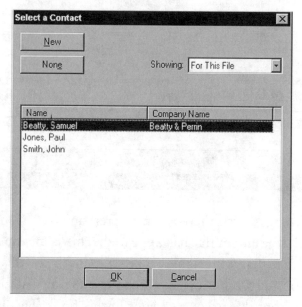

Notice a few things. If this appointment was with someone new, you could click on the New button and create an entry for this person in your Amicus Attorney contact module. Or alternatively, rather than showing only those people "For This File," you could go to the pull-down menu at the top right of the dialog box and ask Amicus to display a different list of people in your Contacts Manager—for example, everyone who is a lawyer. But for our purposes we simply wish to make an appointment with our client, Mr. Smith.

▶ So, double-click on John Smith or click once on his name and then click on "OK." You should find yourself back in the "Event Details" screen as follows:

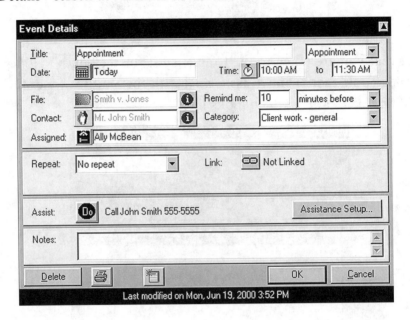

Notice a few things. First, there is a new area on your Event screen: "Assist: [Do] Call John Smith" has appeared. This is an Amicus Attorney shortcut that will enable you to log and track this call. If you were to click on the Do button, then the New Phone Call dialog screen would pop up—but this is covered later in this book. Furthermore, if the appointment was for a purpose other than making a phone call to John Smith, then you could click on "Setup Assistance" to indicate the purpose of this event.

For our purposes, "Assist: [Do] Call John Smith" is just fine.

Second, look at the "Notes" section. This is where you can jot down any reminders to yourself about this meeting. For example, you may wish to discuss a recent report from the surveyor that indicates that the neighbor's tree cutters would necessarily have had to have trespassed 15 feet onto your client's property to remove the trees. Or you could jot down that the Statement of Defense filed by the lawyers for Paul Jones admits a trespass has occurred but denies any damage was suffered by John Smith.

▶ Go ahead and type in any notes that you wish (to do so, click on the Notes box and type in a reminder note to yourself).

Third, notice that Amicus Attorney has a default to automatically remind you of this appointment ten minutes beforehand. You can change this notification time from ten minutes to whatever time period you wish. Amicus Attorney has a range of notification messages—and we will find out how to change these later in the book. My personal favorite is "Peggy"—a very pleasant lady with an English accent that, at the appointed time, will say through your computer's speaker: "Sorry to interrupt, but you have an appointment soon."

*Advanced Tip: Peggy is SO polite and SO professional that I have been known to deliberately make two appointments instead of one. The first appointment is a typical one to remind me of my upcoming in-person appointment. The second is for ten minutes before I wish the first appointment to end—and then I make sure that I set the volume up nice and loud on my computer. If the first appointment drags on and my client is still seated when Peggy announces the second appointment with "Excuse me—but you have an appointment soon," I find that my dawdling client quickly gets the hint and wraps up their business. Amicus Attorney's time magic/management at work! This is also a technique that I demonstrate in my presentations on Amicus Attorney—and it works every time!*

Enough with this new appointment screen.

▶ Click "OK" and we will automatically be taken back to the Calendar. You should see:

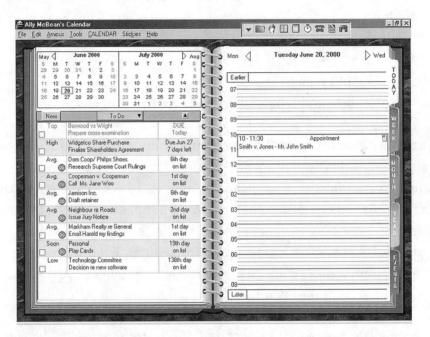

*Advanced Tip: There may now be an hourglass icon appearing in the calendar appointment. Once the time of your appointment is passed, a reminder to do a time entry for the appointment will be displayed by Amicus. If you double-click on this hourglass icon, you will automatically create a time entry for the appointment and Amicus Attorney will complete most of the time entry for you.*

Notice how the appointment is now blocked off in your calendar book. If you went back and opened the Events in the Smith v. Jones file in the Files module, this event would appear there as well. In addition, let's say the appointment start time has changed—from 10 AM to 2 PM.

▶ Click on the appointment and "drag and drop" the appointment to 2 PM. Furthermore, were you to schedule an appointment that over-lapped with this appointment, Amicus would warn you of the con-flict, thereby eliminating the need for you to quickly develop a clone.

Next, we will create a To-Do. There are many ways to create a To-Do entry. From the Calendar screen, notice the listing "To-Do" and the button "New" on the left page of your calendar, which looks like:

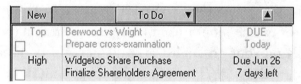

▶ Click on the New button. You should see:

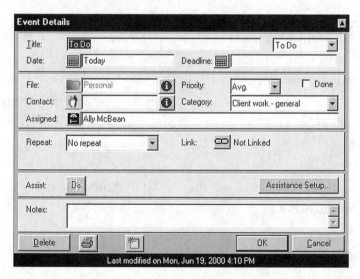

Notice the similarity between the "To-Do" event screen and the "Appointment" event screen. This similarity flattens the learning curve transferring your knowledge quickly due to the commonality of functions.

▶ Now, look at the "Date" and "Deadline" fields. These two parameters allow you to create a To-Do starting today with a deadline of say, one week from now. Alternatively, you can create a To-Do that does not start until one month from now—for example, arising from your meeting with Mr. Smith. He has agreed to assemble a report outlining his losses and damage to his property from his neighbor's trespass, and you must create interrogatories to the Defendant based on his report. You have given your client one month to get the report into you. Therefore, you wish create a To-Do to draw the interrogatories one month from now—and you don't want to have to see daily on your To-Do list over the next thirty days. So you set the start date thirty days away—and forget about it. When the time comes, Amicus will pop it up in your To-Do list.

▶ Now, notice that the words "To-Do" in the "title" are highlighted. You will want to replace them with "Draw Interrogatories" (we could have done the same in our Appointment event window if we had wanted more details for our meeting). In this way, your To-Do will not just say "To-Do" but will say "Draw Interrogatories." You can leave it as "To-Do" if you wish—but why not take advantage of Amicus?

▶ The next step is to click on the calendar symbol next to "Date:" You should see a pop-up calendar that looks like:

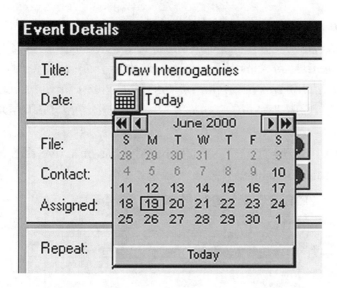

▶ With the mouse, click on the single right arrow that looks like: ▶

Clicking on the single arrow button will move you forward one month (the single left arrow, back one month). The double right arrow button will move you ahead one year (the double left arrow, back one year). So, move ahead to the next month by clicking on the single right arrow button.

▶ Select the business day that is closest to one month from now and click on that date. Notice that the date you selected is now shown in the dialog box. Next, move to "Deadline:" and again click on the Calendar symbol. Let's assume that you give yourself two weeks to complete the interrogatories.

▶ Choose a date that is two weeks after the start date (you may have to move into the next month) and click on it. Notice that this deadline date now appears on the dialog screen.

*Advanced Tip: Another way of doing this is to use the Date Calculator in Amicus Attorney. The Date Calculator is an excellent tool for determining exact dates, such as thirty business days from today. If you wish, the Date Calculator can be found on the drop-down or right-click menu or by pressing "Ctrl," "Shift," and "D" while creating the To-Do.*

▶ Similarly, click on "File:" Notice that the list of active files appears, which should look like:

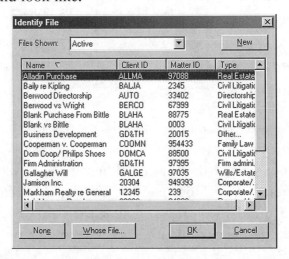

▶ Click on the Smith v. Jones file and then click on "OK" (or alternatively double-click on the file name) and you should be taken back to the To-Do dialog screen. This inserts the file reference into this To-Do.

▶ Next notice the "Notes:" area. By clicking in this area, you can type in a short note to yourself such as "Draw Interrogatories based on the report from John Smith on the damages suffered by him." Just before we click on the "OK" button, your screen should look like:

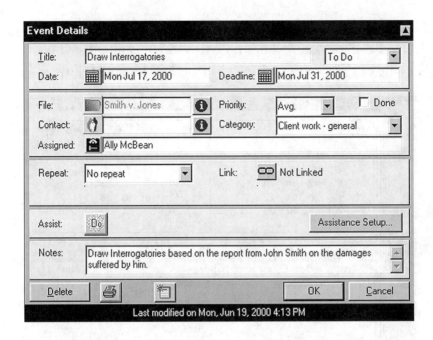

*Advanced Tip: Notice "Link"and "Not Linked." Many of your tasks are dependent on other things happening, and must be done within a certain time frame. Amicus Attorney allows you to chain events (To-Dos and appointments) together and to save them as a "precedent" so they may be reused. For example, this is especially useful for litigation lawyers who must file a defense or answer within a set period of time on receiving a Notice of Claim or Complaint. Setting up these times from receipt of notice of claim to trial is one of the benefits of the linking capability of Amicus.*

▶ Everything fine? Good—then click on "OK." Now we will verify that Amicus has done everything right. We should be at the Calendar screen, looking at today.

▶ Click the day you entered as either the first To-Do date or your
To-Do deadline date. Notice how the To-Do is now listed on the
left-side of the calendar view, which should look as follows:

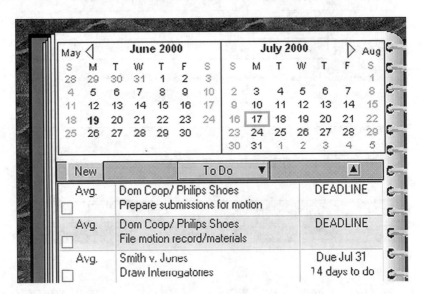

Voila! You now have a To-Do in your calendar that will pop up on the
correct date to remind you to draw the interrogatories on the Smith v.
Jones file. Moreover, it does not appear on today's To-Do list, as it
would be just clutter—it is only meaningful on the dates that you have
chosen and will pop up in the future. In this way, Amicus Attorney
allows you to organize your time and your deadlines, and it allows you
to embed reminders and To-Do's into your calendar. Furthermore, if
you return to the Smith v. Jones file, you will find this To-Do listed
under Events.

Now, let's move on to the next lesson. It covers time tracking, which
allows you to track your billable and non-billable time.

# The Time Sheets
# —Tracking Your Time

There are several ways to track and create time entries within Amicus Attorney.

▶ Let's go back to the Calendar view. (Click on the Calendar icon on your Toolbar or on the Calendar button from your "Office" desktop.)

On the Calendar in the Tutorial Office, there is a To-Do item titled "Widgetco Share Purchase, Finalize Shareholders Agreement." The To-Do will be shown as follows:

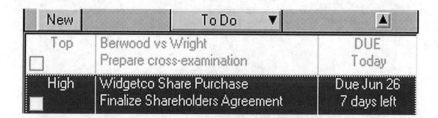

▶ Notice that on the left-hand side of the To-Do there is a small check box. Point and click on the box to mark it "done." If your default Preferences have not been changed, you will be presented with the following:

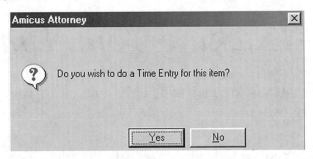

▶ Click on "Yes" and the Time Entry Details screen will appear:

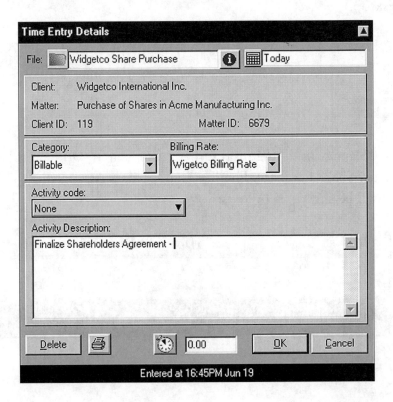

Notice that all the details from your To-Do item have been transferred to the Time Entry Details screen, including the Client and Matter name, Client and Matter ID for your accounting system, and the Activity Description.

You can make changes to any of the these items if necessary.

▶ To complete this time entry, all you have to do is enter the time spent in the box just to the left of the OK button. Click on the box and type over the zeros to enter 1.5. Then click OK.

Several things have happened. On your calendar, your To-Do item is marked "done." In the client's file, the To-Do would show as Done and a Time Entry would appear under Time Spent. Furthermore, the Time Entry has been added to your Daily Time Sheet in Amicus Attorney. Let's go see:

▶ Click on the Time Sheet icon from the toolbar or, alternatively, from the Time Sheets icon from the Office page, which look like:

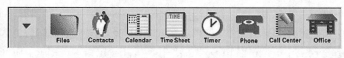

This launches the Time Sheet module that looks like:

*Advanced Tip: If you were to click on the Today button, you would see that Time Sheets are kept for each day. Clicking on "Billable/Non-Billable" shows you that Amicus Attorney tracks both your Billable and Non-billable time. Clicking on the Post button shows you that your daily Time Sheet can be sent electronically to your accounting or billing system.*

Notice several things. First, your time entry for the Widgetco file appears on your "Unposted" list, which is the default view. Most of the time we will be working from the Unposted view. The other views allow you to keep track of your time from a monthly and annual per-spective (to gauge how you are meeting your billing targets) and to search out time entries.

We are going to create a new time entry.

▶ Click on the ⬚ New ⬚ button at the bottom right of the Time Sheet module. You should see the following:

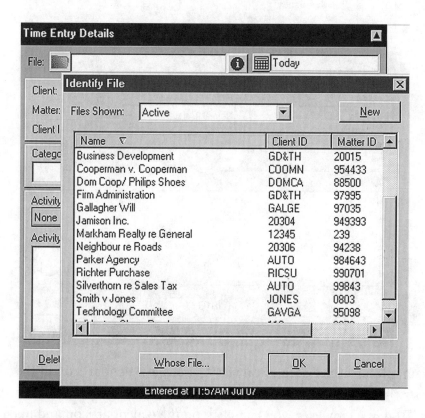

Amicus Attorney wishes to make the time entry as easy as possible—so the Active file list pops up. This gives you the option of making a time entry on an existing file or creating a new file and then posting time on this new file.

▶ Let's double-click on the Smith v. Jones file or, alternatively, click once on Smith v. Jones and then click on "OK."

Notice that Amicus inserts the Smith v. Jones file information into the Time Entry screen which should look like:

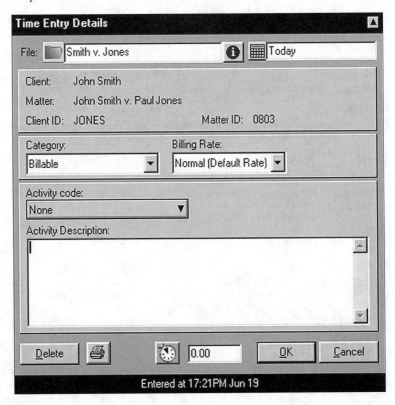

Again, please notice several things. There is a Calendar icon in the upper-right side with "Today" displayed. The default for a time entry is for "Today." However, you can click on the Calendar icon and make an entry for yesterday or some other day as well. For now we will leave the default for "Today."

*Advanced Tip: Notice that you can change the billing rate from "Normal (Default Rate)" to "Premium" or "Contingency" or one of the other pull-down menu selections. For the moment, we will use the Normal (Default Rate).*

Notice the "Activity code" field:

▶ By clicking on the down arrow, a pull-down menu is displayed with a number of common billable descriptions, such as "Consultation with," "Drafting documents," and "Trial Preparations." In our case, since we have done some research preparing for our meeting with our client Mr. Smith, we wish to create a time entry. We click on "Research" from the list that looks like:

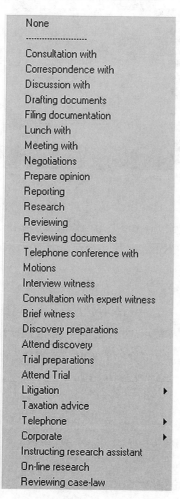

None
-------------------

Consultation with
Correspondence with
Discussion with
Drafting documents
Filing documentation
Lunch with
Meeting with
Negotiations
Prepare opinion
Reporting
Research
Reviewing
Reviewing documents
Telephone conference with
Motions
Interview witness
Consultation with expert witness
Brief witness
Discovery preparations
Attend discovery
Trial preparations
Attend Trial
Litigation                    ▶
Taxation advice
Telephone                     ▶
Corporate                     ▶
Instructing research assistant
On-line research
Reviewing case-law

Notice that "Research" then appears in the Activity/Description area of the Time Entry screen.

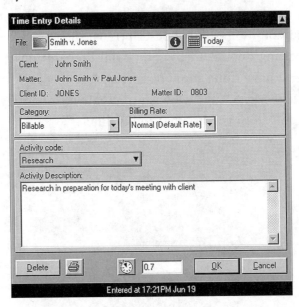

▶ In this case, click on the box and type in the full description of the activities that you performed. In the example above, I have recorded the description of "Research in preparation for today's meeting with client."

*Advanced Tip: At the bottom of the time entry screen is a clock and a time display. You could use Amicus Attorney to time the meeting by opening this screen at the start of your meeting and then clicking on the clock icon. In this way, Amicus would time the activity for you.*

Since we are recording the time following the conclusion of our work, we note that our research lasted .7 of an hour.

▶ Click on the time display and type in "0.7," and then click "OK."

*Advanced Tip: If we had created the time entry from the appointment in the Calendar, the time would have defaulted to the length of the appointment.*

Now you should be taken to the Time Sheet module that displays the completed time entry on the Smith v. Jones file as follows:

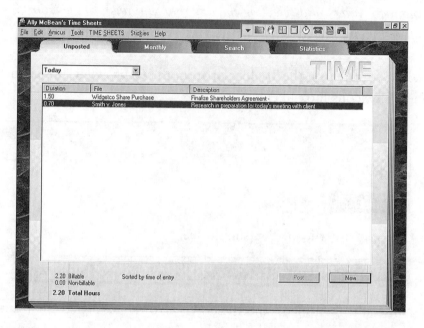

Your time entry for the Smith file has been added to your "Today's" time sheet. Note that your time sheet also contains the time entry for the Widgetco file.

Notice that Amicus Attorney tracks your Billable and Non-Billable time separately and updates the display in this screen as you go. When we opened the Time Module, the time for today was 1.50 hours. Now it is 2.20. It will cumulate your time as you progress through your day. This feature is not found on the major competitors to Amicus Attorney and it is very handy. You have a constant updated total of the billable and non-billable time spent today.

*Advanced Tip: At the top of the screen "Today" is displayed with a pull-down menu. You can refer to time entries for past-days as easily as you can reference the time that you entered today by clicking on the down arrow near Today and selecting the day that you wish to see from the displayed menu list.*

One last feature. On the Toolbar or from the Office view, notice the Timer. The icons look like:

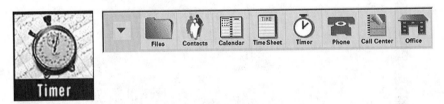

▶ Click on either icon. You should see:

▶ Notice the "Untitled" and the down-arrow. This signals that this is a pull-down menu. Click on the arrow and find Smith v. Jones from the displayed menu list. You should see:

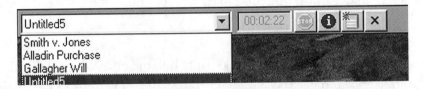

Notice the timer—and how it is working away timing on Smith v. Jones. This is a quick way to start logging your time on any of your files. Moreover, if you are interrupted by a telephone call, click on the Stop icon—this stops the timer on Smith v. Jones. You can then log the time for the telephone call, and then go back to logging time on Smith v. Jones via the Timer. Quick and easy time tracking on the fly! Moreover, you can jump to the Time Sheet at any point in the day and see how your cumulative time totals are coming along.

▶ Remember the tabs on the Time Sheet screen? Click on the Monthly tab:

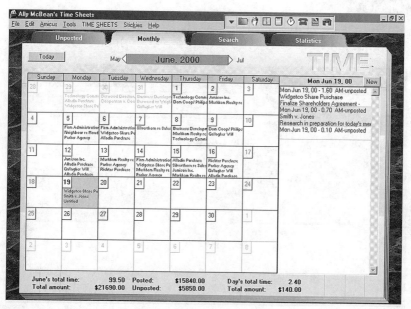

Notice that the display includes not only the daily time total, but also the monthly total as well. Posted and Unposted? These are totals for time that has not yet been sent to the accounting system (unposted) as well as time that has (posted). Needless to say, time should be posted as often as necessary to allow your accounting system to keep accurate time records.

We have just gone through the two most common methods of tracking time in Amicus.

What about telephone calls you say?

▶ OK, click on the telephone icon from either the Toolbar or the Office screen, which look like:

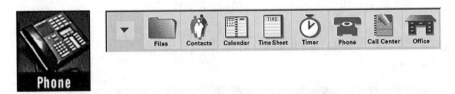

You will be taken to a New Phone Call screen, which looks like:

This is a quick way of not only logging your time on a telephone call, but also for creating a memo for the call that will be stored in Amicus and may be called up at will for review purposes.

Notice that there is a pull-down menu that defaults to "From." A mouse click will convert it to "To" for an outgoing call.

▶ Clicking on the people icon brings up your list of contacts. Type the first few characters of "Beatty" and then choose Samuel Beatty from the list displayed.

▶ Next, clicking on "File" pulls down a menu that brings up the list of files that involve Samuel Beatty. Select "Smith v. Jones." Notice that if you select someone for whom you have entered a phone number in the Contact screen, their phone number automatically appears under the "Phone" area. Having done this you should see:

*Advanced Tip: Clicking on the File or Contact line displays more information on the File or the Contact being referenced. Clicking on the triangle on the Phone line allows you to sift through alternative phone numbers for the contact. Clicking on "Show Calls" allows you to see the notes of previous calls with this person or on this file. Furthermore, if you are networked you can also see the notes of phone calls that others in your firm have made on this file or this contact.*

▶ Now click on the Notes window and type in a memo of your call into the notes area. When complete, click on the Stop button.

*Advanced Tip: The Stop button can also be used if you are interrupted. Clicking it again will resume the timer.*

▶ Since your call is done, click on "Do a Time Entry" and the Time Entry Details screen will appear:

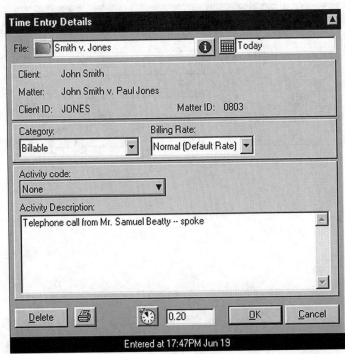

Notice that the time for the call is recorded. It may have defaulted to .20 of an hour, which is a default Preference setting (that you can change) for the minimum time spent on any transaction. The activity description may or may not display the notes you just typed—this is a setting you can change in Preferences. Displayed or not, Amicus has a record of the time.

▶ Click on "OK" to finalize the entry.

*Advanced Tip: You can open a New Phone Call dialog from both the Files and the Contacts Modules. You will notice a telephone icon on each person's business card (whether in a file or on a contact). Clicking on the Telephone icon will cause the phone log dialog screen to appear.*

*Advanced Tip: Another method of tracking a phone call is from the Calendar. If you create a To-Do to call someone, as soon as you choose a contact name for the To-Do, a Do button will appear on the To-Do. Clicking on the Do button will cause the telephone dialog screen to appear. From the Toolbar, click on the Calendar icon. You will notice a To-Do item on your Today view in the Calendar that says to "Call Ms. Jane Woo." Click on the Do button and the phone call dialog screen will appear. Click "Do a Time Entry" and then click "OK" on the time entry. The Do button is another shortcut in Amicus Attorney that provides endless productivity benefits.*

▶ Return to your "Time Sheet" module and notice how your Time Sheet shows the completed telephone call in the list of logged time. Congratulations! You did not have to complete a time sheet to log this call—Amicus Attorney does this automatically. This is part of the integration power of Amicus Attorney, and how it makes logging your time and activities easier than paper-based systems!

# *The Call Center —Managing Your Phone Calls and Messages*

From personal experience I know that I, and most of the other lawyers I know, spend a great deal of time on the telephone. In this lesson you will learn how Amicus Attorney will help you manage your phone calls and make the time you spend on the phone more productive.

The Call Center can be accessed in several ways:

▶ Click on the Call Center icon from the Toolbar or from the Office screen:

Either icon will take you to the Call Center, which looks like:

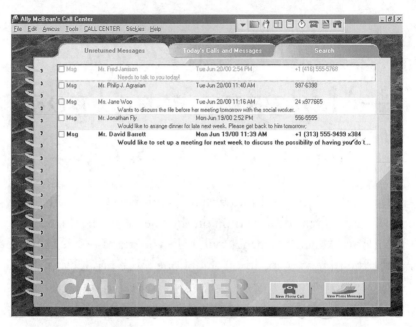

Notice that the Call Center has three tabs: "Unreturned Messages," "Today's Calls and Messages," and "Search." Taking it from the top, let's create a phone message for a call.

▶ Click on the New Phone Message button:

This launches the New Phone Message dialog box:

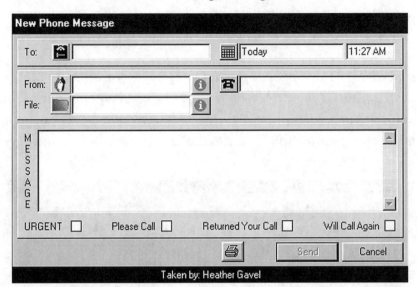

Again, notice how this dialog screen builds on the common tools in Amicus Attorney: the Contacts Manager (for the To: and From: areas) and the Calendar (for the date area). Note that the phone call dialog is similar to the phone message slips that you are accustomed to seeing, except that the message notepad area can take a detailed message.

We will see how each icon brings up a menu of selections. For example, in the "To:" area, you will see the Lawyer icon:

This allows you to select which lawyer to send the message to.

▶ Clicking on the Lawyer icon brings up the list of all the lawyers that are listed either in your Team, in all Groups, or in your Workgroup. Ordinarily you would find the lawyer and double-click on the lawyer's name or click and drag the lawyer name from the left screen to the right screen. Note that since we are in the Tutorial Office, you must choose Tutorial Office as your lawyer.

*Advanced Tip: You can set up a default lawyer for all New Messages under the Call Center tab in Preferences. Your secretary can set his/her default to your name in their Amicus Attorney and YOU can setup your name as the default. This facilitates the recording of messages.*

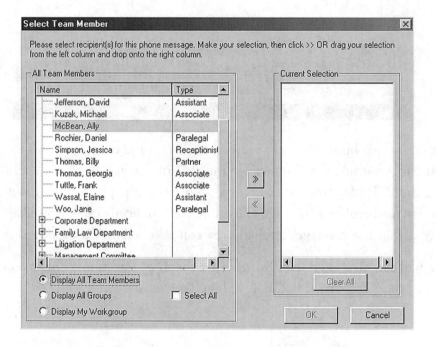

▶ Click on "OK." Notice you are now back in the New Phone Message dialog and the lawyer's name now appears as "Tutorial Office" in the To: area.

▶ Next click on the "From:" icon. Notice that you have been taken to a menu of all of your contacts in your list. Select a contact from the menu (James Hatfield for example) and click on "OK."

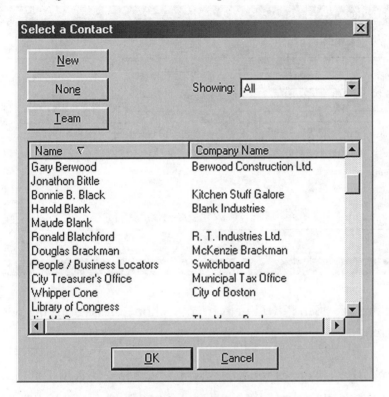

Again, notice that you are back in the Call Center (phone slip) dialog box. Notice also that the contact information, the file (if there was more than one file for James Hatfield, you would click on the File icon to display all the files that he is associated with), and James Hatfield's telephone number all have been automatically inserted into the Phone Message dialog box.

▶ Now type in the text of the phone message and then click in the box indicating "Please Call." Your message slip should now look like:

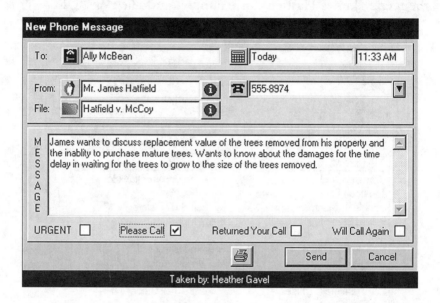

▶ Clicking on "Send" will deliver your phone message to the selected lawyer.

*Advanced Tip: If you had marked the phone slip "Urgent," a "Stickie" message would have been displayed on the recipient's computer screen alerting him or her of the urgent call.*

Also upon clicking "Send," a ringing telephone will be heard and a telephone icon will be placed on the recipient's toolbar. (This will NOT happen in the Tutorial Mode, so be sure to try it when you are back in your own Office.) After sending the message, the "Unreturned Messages" list should look like:

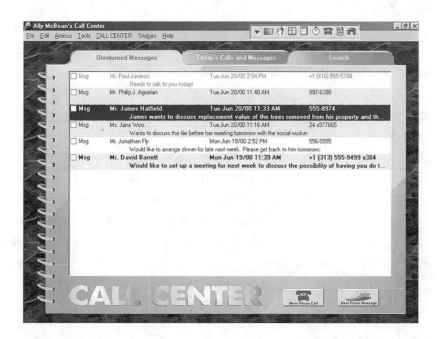

Now we are going to see how Call Center works when you are the person receiving a phone message.

▶ From the Call Center screen (see above), double-click on the message we have just created (note that the phone call message appears in full).

*Advanced Tip: Click on "Forward" to send the call to someone else in your firm (it will then appear in their Call Center) or click on "Make This a To-Do" to schedule returning the call on a specific day in your Calendar.*

▶ To return the call, click on the Phone icon and notice that the New Phone Call screen with all the contact and file information already inserted appears. Notice also that the call timer has started and you are automatically logging the time on this call. After you have completed this phone call, click in the Notes windows to type in your notes on this call.

After entering your notes about the call, you would want to create a time entry.

▶ To do this, click on "Do a Time Entry" and you will see a "Time Entry Details" dialog box appear. Notice that your notes are automatically inserted into the time entry slip. If you didn't select a file, Amicus will prompt you to select a file in order to be able to associate the phone call message to a file.

▶ To finish off the Time Entry, click on "OK."

▶ To close off the phone call, click on "OK." You will be taken back to the Call Center.

Look at the Call Center—you should see that your message, which you just returned, has been removed from your list of "Unreturned Messages."

▶ Now click on the Today's Calls and Messages tab in the Call Center.

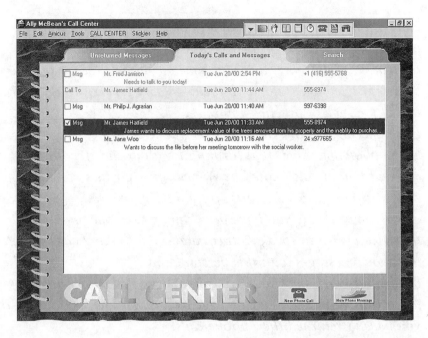

Notice that all messages, as well as the completed and logged calls, are listed under this tab, including your return call to James Hatfield. This Tab allows you to review today's calls quickly and easily.

▶ Double-clicking on any of the entries will bring up the full dialog for you to review rather than the summary displayed. Separating your calls this way keeps you on top of your unreturned messages so that they do not become lost in the shuffle.

*Advanced Tip: The "Search" tab assists you in finding any phone calls or messages for a contact, for all contacts, or for all files within a particular time frame, or for just your unreturned messages. Handling all your messages and phone calls through the Call Center allows you to:*

— *have a complete chronology of all phone communications with a particular person. Open their Contact card or use the "Search" routines in the Call Center and you have a complete record of your game of "telephone tag" with them—a very powerful tool regardless of the type of practice you have;*
— *track and log all your time on your phone calls;*
— *create phone messages that form part of your time record for the day and that are also noted by Amicus on your files;*
— *create To-Do entries that arise from a telephone call;*
— *quickly review why you have been calling someone and what it is that you wished to speak to them about (by looking back through the phone messages with this person); and*
— *be able to search back and determine "who called whom last" when you are met with a challenge by another lawyer or client that you haven't returned their phone calls!*

Onwards to **Putting It All Together**—the chapter that shows how to use Amicus Attorney during the course of your day, from start to finish.

# Putting It All Together —The Sky's the Limit!

In this lesson, we will start with the beginning of your day and apply the Amicus Attorney features already covered in the lessons, together with a few others, to highlight how to use Amicus Attorney as an integrated part of your daily life. In the *Introduction* I gave a glimpse of how you could use Amicus to organize your day. Now that you are familiar with Amicus, we will quickly review how Amicus can be integrated into your practice to give you a head start on immediately reaping the benefits.

You may not use all of the features shown in this chapter. Then again, you may end up using a great deal more—Amicus Attorney is flexible and will go with you as you wish. The point is that you are not a slave to the program. Quite the opposite: Amicus Attorney will serve you in organizing your practice and your day.

So, you come into the office and turn on your computer:

▶ The first thing to do after Windows finishes loading is to launch Amicus Attorney. Your Daily Report is a review of whether or not you have any appointments as well as an opportunity for Amicus Attorney to remind you about certain "housekeeping" matters. One of the housekeeping matters is a reminder that you haven't made any reference to your "To-Do Someday" list. Amicus Attorney maintains two "To-Do" lists. One is your daily list of tasks to be done on files—the standard sort of thing. The other list, the "Do Someday" list, is aimed at capturing those goals that are important but not urgent—and hence get buried in the day-to-day hustle and bustle. The items on your "Do Someday" list? Well, for example, there could be the need to create a new firm brochure, or update the firm Web site. There could be the need to step out of the office and market the practice by giving a lecture to a community group or to a group of clients. There could even be something like creating a list of lifetime goals and a time line to achieve them. Whatever goes into your personal " Do Someday" list is up to you.

▶ You can find the "Do Someday" list by going to the Calendar and clicking on the tab "Events." This will bring up the "Do Someday" list.

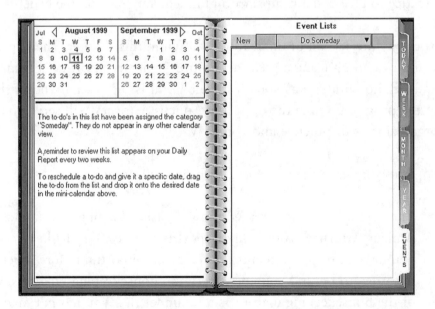

▸ To create an entry in your "Do Someday" list, click on "New."

▸ Complete the entry and click on "OK." The entry now resides in your "Do Someday" list and Amicus Attorney will politely remind you every two weeks to check your list. You can "drag and drop" an entry onto a specific day when you wish to work on one of your personal goals.

Having completed your review of your Daily Report, you decide to check your calendar.

▸ You click on the Calendar icon and the Calendar appears. You look at your appointments and look at your usual To-Do list. You decide to work on one of your To-Do entries (such as call Mr. Smith) at 10:00 AM. Do you create a new appointment? Heavens no!

▸ Simply drag the To-Do entry over to your calendar and drop it at 10:00 AM. The To-Do now becomes an appointment (namely, one with yourself to call Mr. Smith).

Next, check the Call Center to find out what calls have come in and what calls you haven't returned from yesterday. You find that there is a message from Samuel Beatty that he wishes to speak to you regarding a possible settlement of the Smith v. Jones file. You have a choice—you can return the call now—or you can make a To-Do entry in your calendar to call Mr. Beatty back. Do you create a new To-Do? Heavens no!

▶ Right click on the Call Message in Call Center. Notice that a pop-up menu appears.

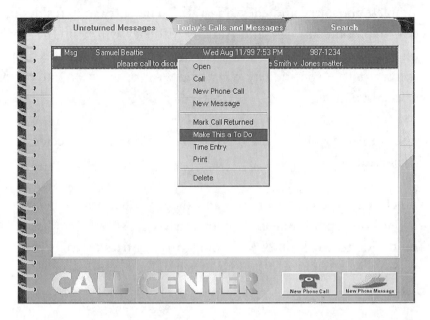

▶ Select "Make This a To-Do." Voila! This message is now in your To-Do list. From here, you can drag and drop it to a time on your calendar, or just leave it as one of your To-Do's today.

You go back to your Daily Report, because it reminded you that you hadn't contacted a specific client for the last sixty days. It is important that you to keep in regular contact with all of your clients, and hence you schedule a time in your calendar to call this client. Likewise, Amicus Attorney reminded you that you hadn't made a time entry on several of your files for the last thirty days. You go to those files in Amicus Attorney and review the log of the past telephone calls. Based on those reviews, you schedule a time in your calendar to call someone on each of the files to move them forward. You also create time entries for these files for reviewing the files, and scheduling further action on them.

▶ Next, you go to the Time Sheet module and click on the Monthly tab. Here you review your billable time for this month and the year's total time. You check to see how you are doing in terms of meeting your billable target for the month.

▶ Need to set your goals? Click on the Statistics tab.

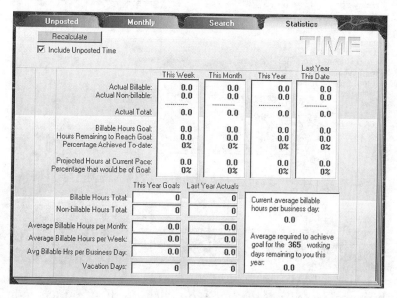

Here you can create your billable goals and average billable hours per month by simply entering your target billable hours total in the area indicated. Amicus Attorney will then calculate your average billable hours per month and average billable hours per week. Enter in last year's totals and Amicus Attorney will do a comparison for you. Moreover, as you enter your billable time in Amicus Attorney, the totals will be updated. This allows you to keep on top of your time without having to contact the Accounting Department and request a report. If everyone in the firm uses Amicus Attorney to track their time, then it is an easy task for the firm administrator to find out how everyone is doing and whether praise or otherwise is needed!

Your phone rings—a potential new client. However, every new client is also a potential conflict of interest. How can you check quickly and easily? You take the call and ask the caller for their full name.

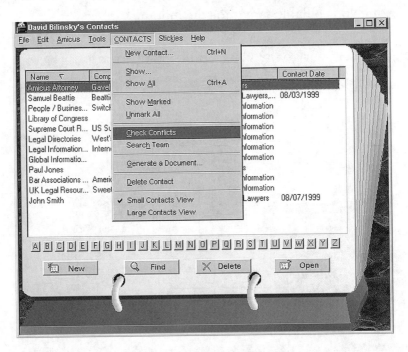

▶ With the caller still on the line, you click on the Contacts icon, then on "CONTACTS", and then on "Check Conflicts." The caller's name happens to be Jones and hence you type in "Jones." Amicus Attorney then pulls up the Paul Jones entry.

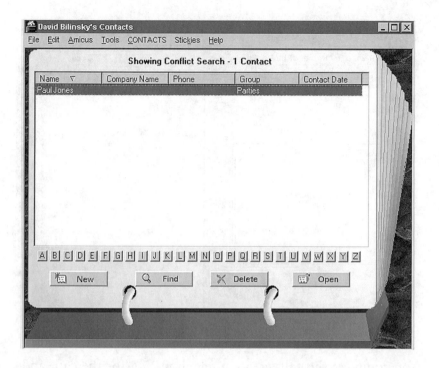

▶ You double-click on "Paul Jones" and ask the caller for his first name and residential address. You determine that the caller is not the Paul Jones of the Smith v. Jones file. Having satisfied yourself that you have no conflicts with Paul Jones (as everyone in the firm uses Amicus Attorney and you have a firm-wide policy to create contact and file entries in Amicus Attorney as soon as possible so that Amicus Attorney is as up-to-date as possible), you take the call.

▶ Along the way, you click on the Files icon and open a new file for the caller. You create a Contact entry for the caller. You type yourself a note regarding the file in the File Summary.

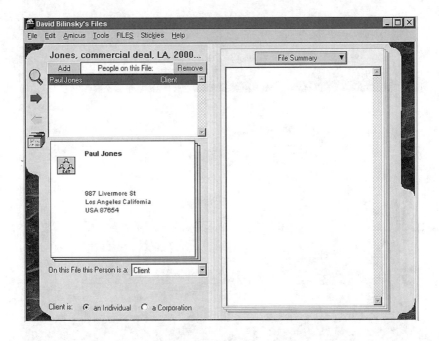

▶ You complete the call, create a telephone log for the call, and complete a time entry for the new file. As you made an appointment for the client to come in and discuss the file, you go to the Calendar and create a new appointment for two days hence. You also create a To-Do on the file.

Completed with this new file, you go back and check your Call Center to see if any calls came in while you were on the telephone. Time to check your email! Now, you could minimize Amicus Attorney and then launch Outlook Express (or whatever email program you are using), but there is another way.

▶ Go to Amicus Attorney Office and click on "Setup," and then "Tools."

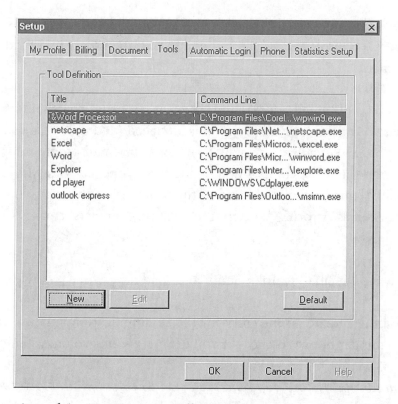

This section of Amicus Attorney allows you to create shortcuts from Amicus Attorney to your most often used applications. In the Tools section above, you can see that I have created shortcuts to WordPerfect, Netscape, Excel, Word, Internet Explorer, the Windows CD-player (I usually work to music played on the computer's sound card), and Outlook Express. Once these shortcuts are made, you can jump to any of them from any part of Amicus Attorney by clicking on "Tools" in the pull-down menu from any part of Amicus Attorney (Contacts, Office, Files, Calendar, Time Sheet etc). Amicus Attorney will then launch the application. Want another shortcut? Remember Mr. John Smith, and that earlier I asked you to enter his email address in his entry in the Contacts section?

▶ Click on "Contacts," then click on "Mr. Smith" and see that his email address is displayed as blue and underlined (the usual "hypertext" link format).

▶ Click on his email address and see what happens. You should find that your default email program is launched (and note that you do not have to create an entry in Tools for your email program for this to work) and the composition dialog box is opened with Mr. John Smith's email address inserted as the recipient. In this way, you can use Amicus Attorney to keep track of your Contacts' email addresses.

You create the email to John Smith and send it.

▶ You then create a time entry for the communication and also create a reminder notice to check if you get a reply in two days' time.

*Advanced Tip: Before you send the email to John Smith, block the text of the email (drag your mouse over the text) and copy it (using the Edit and Copy commands on the menu bar, or right-click over the blocked text). Open a "New Telephone Call" dialog box in Amicus. Paste the copied text of the email into the telephone message area. Just like a telephone call message, insert John Smith into the Contact area, select the appropriate File and in the area for "Phone" type in "email to John Smith." Voila! Now you have a record of the email that will be displayed in the same list as your phone calls with John Smith.*

As your day goes on, you get messages in your Call Center and you return the calls or create Appointments or To-Do's. In each case you track your time and make entries to your Daily Time Sheet. You log all your calls both incoming and outgoing. You check your calendar for your To-Do's and create new ones or mark existing ones as being done. At 11:50 AM "Peggy" speaks to you from your computer and reminds you that you have a lunch appointment scheduled with someone who is meeting you at your office. You straighten out your desk and are ready to go when reception calls you to tell you that your guest has arrived.

▶ Once back in the office, you block off a portion of the afternoon to look after an important file with a deadline that popped up in your To-Do list. You had previously dragged and dropped the entry into your Calendar to create the "appointment" with the file. You turn on the Timer in Amicus Attorney and work away until "Peggy" pipes up and again gently reminds you of another appointment.

Oh boy—you look at your calendar and sigh! This is one appointment that you were not looking forward to. You complete the time entry on the file that you were working on, and just before you go out to reception, you ask yourself how long you need to spend with this next appointment. You decide that twenty minutes would be more than enough time. You create another appointment to start in thirty minutes from now and make sure that "Peggy" will remind you of this later appointment ten minutes beforehand. You go out and collect your client and settle back into your office. Sure enough—the appointment is starting to drag—just as you suspected. No worry—at twenty minutes into the appointment (ten minutes before the next "appointment") "Peggy" comes on and in her most pleasant way reminds you that you have another appointment soon. Voila! Now your client, who would otherwise sit in your office wasting time, realizes that you have someone else coming and quickly gets to the point. Courtesy of Amicus Attorney's early warning system and "Peggy," you have managed your time well and gently eased your difficult client out of the office.

▶ How do you activate "Peggy"? Go to the Amicus Attorney Office screen, click on "Files" and then "Preferences" Once there, click on the tab Calendar and then "Alarms." From the pull-down menu, find "Appointment Reminder (Peggy)."

▶ Click on the Test button and listen to Peggy say, in her wonderful English-accented voice, "Excuse me, but you have an appointment soon." Voila! You need never have to sit and wish you had an easy way to end an appointment again!

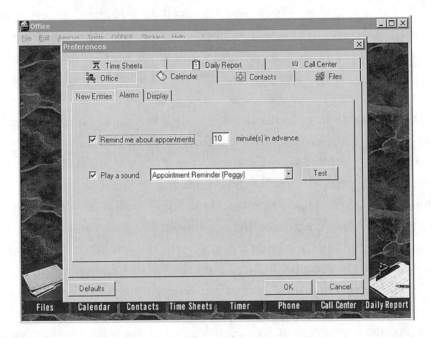

As you progress during the day, you will open new files, create new contact entries and associate them with new or existing files. You will track your time and generate letters and fax cover sheets. Moreover, when it is time to start cleaning up your desk and organizing yourself for tomorrow, dear Peggy will remind you that you have an appointment with yourself to start preparing to leave. You can drag unfinished business to tomorrow, return any calls that have been left and print out your time sheet (to serve as a backup in case accounting crashes their system!). You are ahead of the game and ready to dig in tomorrow. You leave the office knowing that you made the best of your time and your energy. Time to relax and enjoy the rest of your day!

## The Sky's the Limit!

There are many other features of Amicus Attorney that we haven't explored. There are other settings that could be changed, settings that could be modified. Amicus Attorney is both powerful and easy to use. The purpose of this book is to introduce you to Amicus Attorney and allow you to start using Amicus Attorney quickly and easily. Most of the ease of use is due to the user-friendly interface—one of the strengths of Amicus Attorney. The other strength is the file-oriented approach that Amicus Attorney uses to organize the different components of the software. These two factors have made Amicus Attorney the most widely used legal case manager in existence. I hope that this book has met your needs in terms of allowing you to tap into Amicus Attorney' potential for you and your practice. In preparing for a revised edition of this book, your thoughts and comments and suggestions are welcome. Please email me at dbilinsky@lsbc.org.

# Document Generation

## Using Word and WordPerfect

Welcome to the automatic document generation abilities of Amicus Attorney. Amicus Attorney can automatically produce documents for you using the information in Contacts Manager. Before we can start generating documents, there are some housekeeping matters to which we must attend.

To use Microsoft Word 97 or later in generating documents from Amicus Attorney, you need the components that are placed on your hard drive by the Typical install option. If you selected any other installation option when you originally installed Word, you must run the Setup program again and select the Typical install option.

If you are using Word 2000, you must set the macro security level to either Medium or Low. Setting macro security to a setting of High will not allow any of the Amicus Attorney document assembly macros to run. Refer to the Word 2000 documentation for instructions on setting the macro security level.

To use Corel WordPerfect 7 or later in generating documents from Amicus Attorney, you need to set up WordPerfect so that three special buttons will appear in its toolbar. Here's how:

After installing Amicus Attorney, start WordPerfect. From the Tools menu, choose Macro, then choose Play. A dialog box then appears.

From the "Look in" drop-down list, choose the drive (probably C:/) in where you installed Amicus Attorney. Open the folder called "Amimerge." Select the WordPerfect macro called Aawptlbr.WCM, then click Play.

Now switch back to Amicus Attorney (did you keep your Toolbar on top?).

▶ Click on the Contacts icon from the Toolbar or from the Office screen.

You should see your list of contacts. Note the pull-down menus across the top of the screen with headings: File, Edit, Amicus, Tools, CONTACTS, Stickies and Help.

*User Tip: This setup can be done from any of the modules. We have picked the Contact Manager as we will first generate a document from this module.*

▶ Click on File.

▶ From the list of menu options, click on Setup.

Now, notice the setup screen. This is how it would look in your own "Office." In the Tutorial Office there are less options.

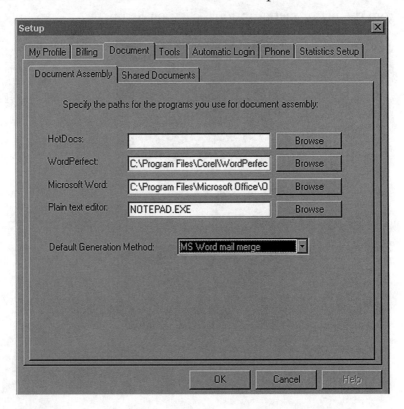

▶ Click on the "Document" tab. Now we need to know where WINWORD.EXE and/or WPWIN9.EXE (depending on whether you use Word or WordPerfect) reside on your hard drive in order to tell Amicus where to find them.

In my case, WordPerfect is found on C:\Program Files\Corel\WordPerfect Office 2000\programs\wpwin9.exe. If you are using an earlier version of WordPerfect, then your copy will probably be located elsewhere. (Hint: Launch Explorer, and using Find, search for WPWIN. You should find WPWIN8.exe).

On my system, Word was found at C:\Program Files\Microsoft Office\ Office\winword.exe.

▶ Use the Browse button to search for these files. Then use the Default Generation Method to indicate whether you use WordPerfect or Word. For the purposes of this chapter, we will use Word Merge Files.

▶ When you have provided Amicus with the paths to your word processor and specified the Default Generation Method, click on "OK." Now we are ready to start generating documents!

For the purposes of this lesson, we will be generating a letter from the Contacts Manager.

▶ From the index of the Contacts, find Samuel Beatty and double-click on his entry (or click once on his entry and click on "Open").

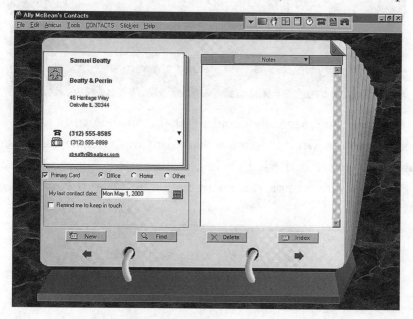

Notice the pull-down menu of "File Edit Amicus Tools CONTACTS Stickies Help"

▶ Click on "CONTACTS" and find the menu selection "Generate a Document." Click on it.

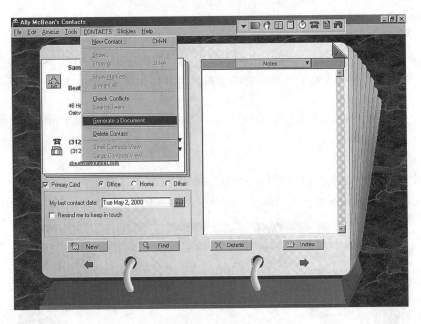

This will launch the menu of documents that Amicus Attorney will produce for you in Word (assuming that Word was your default generation method selected earlier). To help get you started, Amicus Attorney is shipped with several sample document templates for both WordPerfect and Word.

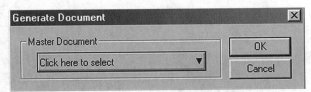

▶ Click on the down arrow to bring up the menu of selections.

▶ Click on "Letters," then on "Blank Letter" and then on "OK."
What you should see is the Word screen with the Amicus Attorney
merge letter:

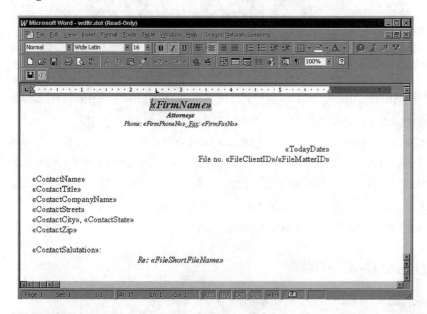

Now notice the Amicus Attorney symbol that appears in the
WordPerfect Toolbar on the left side of your screen:

The <F> icon—shows a list of all the fields in Amicus Attorney and is
used to create a template or Master Document.

The Amicus Attorney icon will merge the information from your contact in Amicus Attorney into your document.

▶ Click on the Amicus Attorney icon. Notice that a Save dialog box appears:

▶ For the moment, click on "Don't Save and Don't Attach to Brad Page"(a brad is a collection of documents held together by a clip. Amicus Attorney has brad pages that bring together data on files. For documents, it allows you to index all the documents you produce for a file. We looked at these pages in an earlier lesson. For our purposes, we need not save the precedent nor attach it to the brad page in Amicus Attorney).

▶ Then click on "OK."

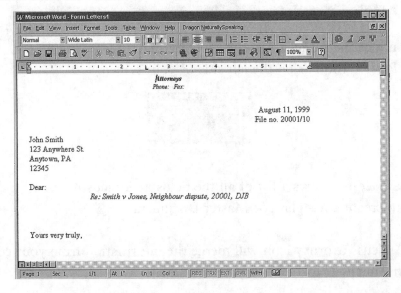

Voila! You have generated a blank letter directly from Amicus Attorney courtesy of WordPerfect or Word. You can take it a step further by modifying the Master Document form to match your office stationary or your office letter format. Regardless, you have seen how to use Amicus Attorney to produce merged documents from your Contact list. By exploring the list of documents that come with Amicus Attorney, you can see that you can generate a number of documents, from office-related documents (files index, status reports, contact index—address and phone etc.), file-oriented documents (retainer letters, overdue account reminders, client letters) to practice-oriented documents (power of attorney, affidavit of documents etc.). The ability to create new forms exists by using either Word's or WordPerfect's merge capability, or by using HOTDOCS, which is a document automation program by a company called Capsoft. The document generation feature extends the power of Amicus Attorney, and allows you to further organize your work day and work product around Amicus Attorney.

# Keyboard Shortcuts in Amicus Attorney

## Universal Shortcuts

| | |
|---|---|
| Files | Control-Shift-F |
| Contacts | Control-Shift-N |
| Calendar | Control-Shift-C |
| Time Sheets | Control-Shift-S |
| Call Center | Control-Shift-L |
| Phone Call | Control-Shift-P |
| Timer | Control-Shift-T |
| Master Schedule | Control-Shift-A |
| Office Window | Control-Shift-O |
| Office Toolbar | Control-Shift-B |
| Daily Report | Control-Shift-R |
| Date Calculator | Control-Shift-D |
| To Open the File Menu | Alt-F |
| To Open the Edit Menu | Alt-E |
| To Open the Tools Menu | Alt-T |
| To Open the Stickies Menu | Alt-K |
| To Open the Help Menu | Alt-H |

Press the Down Arrow key repeatedly until the desired command or menu item is highlighted, then press Enter.

## Miscellaneous

| | |
|---|---|
| Print Options | Control-P |
| To Delete an item | press Delete |
| To insert a time stamp into a text box | Control-T |
| To view onscreen help | F1 |

## Office Shortcuts

| | |
|---|---|
| To view onscreen help | F1 |
| To open the Office menu in Organizer, to open the | Alt-O |
| Import menu | Alt-I |
| In Organizer, to open the database | Alt-D |

Press the Down Arrow key repeatedly until the desired command or menu item is highlighted, then press Enter.

## Files Shortcuts (from within the Files Module)

| | |
|---|---|
| To create a new file | Control-N |
| To fine files | Control-F |

## Contacts Shortcuts (from within the Contacts Module)

| | |
|---|---|
| To add a new contact | Control-N |
| To show all contacts | Control-A |
| To find contacts | Control-F |

## Calendar Shortcuts (from within the Calendar Module)

| | |
|---|---|
| To create a new event | Control-N |
| To fine calendar items | Control-F |

## Time Sheets Shortcuts (from within the Time Sheets Module)

| | |
|---|---|
| To create a new time entry | Control-N |
| To find time entries | Control-F |

## Call Center Shortcuts (from within the Call Center Module)

| | |
|---|---|
| To create a new phone call | Control-Shift-P |
| To create a new phone message | Control-Shift-M |

**The ABA Guide to International Business Negotiations.** Explains national, legal, and cultural issues you must consider when negotiating with members of different countries. Includes details of 17 specific countries/nationalities.

**The ABA Guide to Lawyer Trust Accounts.** Details ways that lawyers should manage trust accounts to comply with ethical & statutory requirements.

**The ABA Guide to Legal Marketing.** 14 articles—written by marketing experts, practicing lawyers, and law firm marketing administrators—share their innovative methods for competing in an aggressive marketplace.

**The ABA Guide to Professional Managers in the Law Office.** Shows how lawyers can practice more efficiently by delegating management tasks to professional managers.

**Anatomy of a Law Firm Merger.** Considering a merger? Here's a roadmap that shows how to: determine the costs/benefits of a merger, assess merger candidates, integrate resources and staff, and more.

**Billing Innovations.** Explains how billing and pricing are affect strategic planning, maintaining quality of services, marketing, instituting a compensation system, and firm governance.

**Changing Jobs, 3rd Edition.** A handbook designed to help lawyers make changes in their professional careers. Includes career planning advice from dozens of experts.

**Compensation Plans for Law Firms, 2nd Ed.** This second edition discusses the basics for a fair and simple compensation system for partners, of counsel, associates, paralegals, and staff.

**The Complete Internet Handbook for Lawyers.** A thorough orientation to the Internet, including e-mail, search engines, conducting research and marketing on the Internet, publicizing a Web site, Net ethics, security, viruses, and more. Features a updated, companion Web site with forms you can download and customize.

**Computer-Assisted Legal Research: A Guide to Successful Online Searching.** Covers the fundamentals of LEXIS®-NEXIS® and WESTLAW®, including practical information such as: logging on and off; formulating your search; reviewing results; modifying a query; using special features; downloading documents.

**Computerized Case Management Systems.** Thoroughly evaluates 35 leading case management software applications, helping you pick which is best for your firm.

**Connecting with Your Client.** Written by a psychologist, therapist, and legal consultant, this book presents communications techniques that will help ensure client cooperation and satisfaction.

**Do-It-Yourself Public Relations.** A hands-on guide (and diskette!) for lawyers with public relations ideas, sample letters, and forms.

**Easy Self-Audits for the Busy Law Office.** Dozens of evaluation tools help you determine what's working (and what's not) in your law office or legal department. You'll discover several opportunities for improving productivity and efficiency along the way!

**Finding the Right Lawyer.** Answers the questions people should ask when searching for legal counsel. Includes a glossary of legal specialties and the 10 questions to ask before hiring a lawyer.

**Flying Solo: A Survival Guide for the Solo Lawyer, 2nd Ed.** An updated guide to the issues unique to the solo practitioner.

**Handling Personnel Issues in the Law Office.** Packed with tips on "safely" and legally recruiting, hiring, training, managing, and terminating employees.

**HotDocs® in One Hour for Lawyers.** Offers simple instructions, ranging from generating a document from a template to inserting conditional text and creating custom dialogs.

**How to Build and Manage an Employment Law Practice.** Provides clear guidance and valuable tips for solo or small employment law practices, including preparation, marketing, accepting cases, and managing workload and finances. Includes several time-saving "fill in the blank" forms.

**How to Build and Manage an Estates Law Practice.** Provides the tools and guidance you'll need to start or improve an estates law practice, including

**How to Build and Manage a Personal Injury Practice.** Features all of the tactics, technology, and tools needed for a profitable practice, including hot to: write a sound business plan, develop a financial forecast, choose office space, market your practice, and more.

**How to Draft Bills Clients Rush to Pay.** Dozens of ways to draft bills that project honesty, competence, fairness and value.

**How to Start and Build a Law Practice, Millennium 4th Edition.** Jay Foonberg's classic guide has been completely updated and expanded! Features 128 chapters, including 30 new ones, that reveal secrets to successful planning, marketing, billing, client relations, and much more. Chock-full of forms, sample letters, and checklists, including a sample business plan, "The Foonberg Law Office Management Checklist," and more.

**Internet Fact Finder for Lawyers.** Shares all of the secrets, shortcuts, and realities of conducting research on the Net, including how to tap into Internet sites for investigations, depositions, and trial presentations.

**Law Firm Partnership Guide: Getting Started.** Examines the most important issues you must consider to ensure your partnership's success, including self-assessment, organization structure, written agreements, financing, and basic operations. Includes *A Model Partnership Agreement* on diskette.

## TO ORDER CALL TOLL-FREE:
## 1-800-285-2221

## VISIT OUR WEB SITE:
## http://www.abanet.org/lpm/catalog

**Law Firm Partnership Guide: Strengthening Your Firm.** Addresses what to do after your firm is up and running, including how to handle: change, financial problems, governance issues, compensating firm owners, and leadership.

**Law Law Law on the Internet.** Presents the most influential law-related Web sites. Features Web site reviews of the *National Law Journal's 250*, so you can save time surfing the Net and quickly find the information you need.

**Law Office Policy and Procedures Manual, 3rd Ed.** A model for law office policies and procedures (includes diskette). Covers law office organization, management, personnel policies, financial management, technology, and communications systems.

**Law Office Staff Manual for Solos and Small Firms.** Use this manual as is or customize it using the book's diskette. Includes general office policies on confidentiality, employee compensation, sick leave, sexual harassment, billing, and more.

**The Lawyer's Guide to Creating Web Pages.** A practical guide that clearly explains HTML, covers how to design a Web site, and introduces Web-authoring tools.

**The Lawyer's Guide to the Internet.** A guide to what the Internet is (and isn't), how it applies to the legal profession, and the different ways it can—and should—be used.

**The Lawyer's Guide to Marketing on the Internet.** This book talks about the pluses and minuses of marketing on the Internet, as well as how to develop an Internet marketing plan.

**The Lawyer's Quick Guide to E-Mail.** Covers basic and intermediate topics, including setting up an e-mail program, sending messages, managing received messages, using mailing lists, security, and more.

**The Lawyer's Quick Guide to Microsoft® Internet Explorer; The Lawyer's Quick Guide to Netscape® Navigator.** These two guides de-mystify the most popular Internet browsers. Four quick and easy lessons include: Basic Navigation, Setting a Bookmark, Browsing with a Purpose, and Keeping What You Find.

**The Lawyer's Quick Guide to Timeslips®.** Filled with practical examples, this guide uses three short, interactive lessons to show to efficiently use Timeslips.

**The Lawyer's Quick Guide to WordPerfect® 7.0/8.0 for Windows®.** Covers multitasking, entering and editing text, formatting letters, creating briefs, and more. Includes a diskette with practice exercises and word templates.

**Leaders' Digest: A Review of the Best Books on Leadership.** This book will help you find the best books on leadership to help you achieve extraordinary and exceptional leadership skills.

**Living with the Law: Strategies to Avoid Burnout and Create Balance.** Examines ways to manage stress, make the practice of law more satisfying, and improve client service.

**Marketing Success Stories.** This collection of anecdotes provides an inside look at how successful lawyers market themselves, their practice specialties, their firms, and their profession.

**Microsoft® Word for Windows® in One Hour for Lawyers.** Uses four easy lessons to help you prepare, save, and edit a basic document in Word.

**Practicing Law Without Clients: Making a Living as a Freelance Lawyer.** Describes freelance legal researching, writing, and consulting opportunities that are available to lawyers.

**Quicken® in One Hour for Lawyers.** With quick, concise instructions, this book explains the basics of Quicken and how to use the program to detect and analyze financial problems.

**Risk Management.** Presents practical ways to asses your level of risk, improve client services, and avoid mistakes that can lead to costly malpractice claims, civil liability, or discipline. Includes Law Firm Quality/In Control (QUIC) Surveys on diskette and other tools to help you perform a self-audit.

**Running a Law Practice on a Shoestring.** Offers a crash course in successful entrepreneurship. Features money-saving tips on office space, computer equipment, travel, furniture, staffing, and more.

**Successful Client Newsletters.** Written for lawyers, editors, writers, and marketers, this book can help you to start a newsletter from scratch, redesign an existing one, or improve your current practices in design, production, and marketing.

**Survival Guide for Road Warriors.** A guide to using a notebook computer (laptop) and other technology to improve your productivity in your office, on the road, in the courtroom, or at home.

**Telecommuting for Lawyers.** Discover methods for implementing a successful telecommuting program that can lead to increased productivity, improved work product, higher revenues, lower overhead costs, and better communications. Addressing both law firms and telecommuters, this guide covers start-up, budgeting, setting policies, selecting participants, training, and technology.

**Through the Client's Eyes.** Includes an overview of client relations and sample letters, surveys, and self-assessment questions to gauge your client relations acumen.

**Time Matters® in One Hour for Lawyers.** Employs quick, easy lessons to show you how to: add contacts, cases, and notes to Time Matters; work with events and the calendar; and integrate your data into a case management system that suits your needs.

**Wills, Trusts, and Technology.** Reveals why you should automate your estates practice; identifies what should be automated; explains how to select the right software; and helps you get up and running with the software you select.

**Win-Win Billing Strategies.** Prepared by a blue-ribbon ABA task force of practicing lawyers, corporate counsel, and management consultants, this book explores what constitutes "value" and how to bill for it. You'll understand how to get fair compensation for your work and communicate and justify fees to cost-conscious clients.

**Women Rainmakers' 101+ Best Marketing Tips.** A collection of over 130 marketing from women rainmakers throughout the country. Features tips on image, networking, public relations, and advertising.

**Year 2000 Problem and the Legal Profession.** In clear, nontechnical terms, this book will help you identify, address, and meet the challenges that Y2K poses to the legal industry.

**TO ORDER CALL TOLL-FREE:**
**1-800-285-2221**

| Qty | Title | LPM Price | Regular Price | Total |
|---|---|---|---|---|
| _____ | ABA Guide to International Business Negotiations (5110331) | $ 74.95 | $ 84.95 | $_____ |
| _____ | ABA Guide to Lawyer Trust Accounts (5110374) | 69.95 | 79.95 | $_____ |
| _____ | ABA Guide to Legal Marketing (5110341) | 69.95 | 79.95 | $_____ |
| _____ | ABA Guide to Prof. Managers in the Law Office (5110373) | 69.95 | 79.95 | $_____ |
| _____ | Anatomy of a Law Firm Merger (5110310) | 24.95 | 29.95 | $_____ |
| _____ | Billing Innovations (5110366) | 124.95 | 144.95 | $_____ |
| _____ | Changing Jobs, 3rd Ed. | *please call for information* | | $_____ |
| _____ | Compensation Plans for Lawyers, 2nd Ed. (5110353) | 69.95 | 79.95 | $_____ |
| _____ | Complete Internet Handbook for Lawyers (5110413) | 39.95 | 49.95 | $_____ |
| _____ | Computer-Assisted Legal Research (5110388) | 69.95 | 79.95 | $_____ |
| _____ | Computerized Case Management Systems (5110409) | 39.95 | 49.95 | $_____ |
| _____ | Connecting with Your Client (5110378) | 54.95 | 64.95 | $_____ |
| _____ | Do-It-Yourself Public Relations (5110352) | 69.95 | 79.95 | $_____ |
| _____ | Easy Self Audits for the Busy Law Firm | *please call for information* | | $_____ |
| _____ | Finding the Right Lawyer (5110339) | 14.95 | 14.95 | $_____ |
| _____ | Flying Solo, 2nd Ed. (5110328) | 29.95 | 34.95 | $_____ |
| _____ | Handling Personnel Issues in the Law Office (5110381) | 59.95 | 69.95 | $_____ |
| _____ | HotDocs® in One Hour for Lawyers (5110403) | 29.95 | 34.95 | $_____ |
| _____ | How to Build and Manage an Employment Law Practice (5110389) | 44.95 | 54.95 | $_____ |
| _____ | How to Build and Manage an Estates Law Practice | *please call for information* | | $_____ |
| _____ | How to Build and Manage a Personal Injury Practice (5110386) | 44.95 | 54.95 | $_____ |
| _____ | How to Draft Bills Clients Rush to Pay (5110344) | 39.95 | 49.95 | $_____ |
| _____ | How to Start & Build a Law Practice, Millennium Fourth Edition (5110415) | 47.95 | 54.95 | $_____ |
| _____ | Internet Fact Finder for Lawyers (5110399) | 34.95 | 39.95 | $_____ |
| _____ | Law Firm Partnership Guide: Getting Started (5110363) | 64.95 | 74.95 | $_____ |
| _____ | Law Firm Partnership Guide: Strengthening Your Firm (5110391) | 64.95 | 74.95 | $_____ |
| _____ | Law Law Law on the Internet (5110400) | 34.95 | 39.95 | $_____ |
| _____ | Law Office Policy & Procedures Manual (5110375) | 99.95 | 109.95 | $_____ |
| _____ | Law Office Staff Manual for Solos & Small Firms (5110361) | 49.95 | 59.95 | $_____ |
| _____ | Lawyer's Guide to Creating Web Pages (5110383) | 54.95 | 64.95 | $_____ |
| _____ | Lawyer's Guide to the Internet (5110343) | 24.95 | 29.95 | $_____ |
| _____ | Lawyer's Guide to Marketing on the Internet (5110371) | 54.95 | 64.95 | $_____ |
| _____ | Lawyer's Quick Guide to E-Mail (5110406) | 34.95 | 39.95 | $_____ |
| _____ | Lawyer's Quick Guide to Microsoft Internet® Explorer (5110392) | 24.95 | 29.95 | $_____ |
| _____ | Lawyer's Quick Guide to Netscape® Navigator (5110384) | 24.95 | 29.95 | $_____ |
| _____ | Lawyer's Quick Guide to Timeslips® (5110405) | 34.95 | 39.95 | $_____ |
| _____ | Lawyer's Quick Guide to WordPerfect® 7.0/8.0 (5110395) | 34.95 | 39.95 | $_____ |
| _____ | Leaders' Digest (5110356) | 49.95 | 59.95 | $_____ |
| _____ | Living with the Law (5110379) | 59.95 | 69.95 | $_____ |
| _____ | Marketing Success Stories (5110382) | 79.95 | 89.95 | $_____ |
| _____ | Microsoft® Word for Windows® in One Hour for Lawyers (5110358) | 19.95 | 29.95 | $_____ |
| _____ | Practicing Law Without Clients (5110376) | 49.95 | 59.95 | $_____ |
| _____ | Quicken® in One Hour for Lawyers (5110380) | 19.95 | 29.95 | $_____ |
| _____ | Risk Management (5610123) | 69.95 | 79.95 | $_____ |
| _____ | Running a Law Practice on a Shoestring (5110387) | 39.95 | 49.95 | $_____ |
| _____ | Successful Client Newsletters (5110396) | 39.95 | 44.95 | $_____ |
| _____ | Survival Guide for Road Warriors (5110362) | 24.95 | 29.95 | $_____ |
| _____ | Telecommuting for Lawyers (5110401) | 39.95 | 49.95 | $_____ |
| _____ | Through the Client's Eyes (5110337) | 69.95 | 79.95 | $_____ |
| _____ | Time Matters® in One Hour for Lawyers (5110402) | 29.95 | 34.95 | $_____ |
| _____ | Wills, Trusts, and Technology (5430377) | 74.95 | 84.95 | $_____ |
| _____ | Win-Win Billing Strategies (5110304) | 89.95 | 99.95 | $_____ |
| _____ | Women Rainmakers' 101+ Best Marketing Tips (5110336) | 14.95 | 19.95 | $_____ |
| _____ | Year 2000 Problem and the Legal Profession (5110410) | 24.95 | 29.95 | $_____ |

**\*Handling**
$10.00-$24.99......................$3.95
$25.00-$49.99......................$4.95
$50.00+ $5.95   MD residents add 5%

**\*\*Tax**
DC residents add 5.75%
IL residents add 8.75%

| | |
|---|---|
| Subtotal | $_____ |
| *Handling | $_____ |
| **Tax | $_____ |
| TOTAL | $_____ |

## PAYMENT

☐ Check enclosed (to the ABA)  ☐ Bill Me
☐ Visa  ☐ MasterCard  ☐ American Express

_____
Account Number      Exp. Date      Signature

Name _____ Firm _____
Address _____
City _____ State _____ Zip _____
Phone Number _____ E-Mail Address _____

**Mail: ABA Publication Orders, P.O. Box 10892, Chicago, Illinois 60610-0892 ♦ Phone: (800) 285-2221 ♦ FAX: (312) 988-5568**

**E-Mail: abasvcctr@abanet.org ♦ Internet: http://www.abanet.org/lpm/catalog**

Source Code: 22AEND499

 THE SECTION OF
LAW PRACTICE
MANAGEMENT

# CUSTOMER COMMENT FORM

 ABA

Title of Book: _____

We've tried to make this publication as useful, accurate, and readable as possible. Please take 5 minutes to tell us if we succeeded. Your comments and suggestions will help us improve our publications. Thank you!

1. How did you acquire this publication:

☐ by mail order     ☐ at a meeting/convention     ☐ as a gift

☐ by phone order     ☐ at a bookstore     ☐ don't know

☐ other: (describe) _____

Please rate this publication as follows:

|  | Excellent | Good | Fair | Poor | Not Applicable |
|---|---|---|---|---|---|
| **Readability**: Was the book easy to read and understand? | ☐ | ☐ | ☐ | ☐ | ☐ |
| **Examples/Cases**: Were they helpful, practical? Were there enough? | ☐ | ☐ | ☐ | ☐ | ☐ |
| **Content**: Did the book meet your expectations? Did it cover the subject adequately? | ☐ | ☐ | ☐ | ☐ | ☐ |
| **Organization and clarity**: Was the sequence of text logical? Was it easy to find what you wanted to know? | ☐ | ☐ | ☐ | ☐ | ☐ |
| **Illustrations/forms/checklists**: Were they clear and useful? Were there enough? | ☐ | ☐ | ☐ | ☐ | ☐ |
| **Physical attractiveness**: What did you think of the appearance of the publication (typesetting, printing, etc.)? | ☐ | ☐ | ☐ | ☐ | ☐ |

Would you recommend this book to another attorney/administrator? ☐ Yes ☐ No

How could this publication be improved? What else would you like to see in it?

_____
_____
_____

Do you have other comments or suggestions? _____
_____
_____

Name _____

Firm/Company _____

Address _____

City/State/Zip _____

Phone _____

Firm Size: _____ Area of specialization: _____

**We appreciate your time and help.**

**Fold**

NO POSTAGE
NECESSARY
IF MAILED
IN THE
UNITED STATES

## BUSINESS REPLY MAIL
FIRST CLASS     PERMIT NO. 16471     CHICAGO, ILLINOIS

*POSTAGE WILL BE PAID BY ADDRESSEE*

AMERICAN BAR ASSOCIATION
PPM, 8th FLOOR
750 N. LAKE SHORE DRIVE
CHICAGO, ILLINOIS 60611–9851

**Fold**

**AMERICAN BAR ASSOCIATION**

# ABA Law Practice Management Section

*Membership Application*

## Access to all these information resources and discounts – for just $3.33 a month!

Membership dues are just $40 a year – just $3.33 a month.
You probably spend more on your general business magazines and newspapers.
But they can't help you succeed in building and managing your practice
like a membership in the ABA Law Practice Management Section.
Make a small investment in success. Join today!

**☑ Yes!** I want to join the ABA Section of Law Practice Management Section and gain access to information helping me add more clients, retain and expand business with current clients, and run my law practice more efficiently and competitively!

## Check the dues that apply to you:

❏ $40 for ABA members     ❏ $5 for ABA Law Student Division members

## Choose your method of payment:

❏ Check enclosed (make payable to American Bar Association)
❏ Bill me
❏ Charge to my:     ❏ VISA®     ❏ MASTERCARD®     ❏ AMEX®

Card No.: _____     Exp. Date: _____

Signature: _____     Date: _____

ABA I.D.*: _____
*(∗ Please note: Membership in ABA is a prerequisite to enroll in ABA Sections.)*

Name: _____

Firm/Organization: _____

Address: _____

City/State/ZIP: _____

Telephone No.: _____     Fax No.: _____

Primary Email Address: _____

### Save time by Faxing or Phoning!

**Get Ahead.** 🏃

**ABA** Law Practice Management Section

▶ Fax your application to: (312) 988-5820
▶ Join by phone if using a credit card: (800) 285-2221 (ABA1)
▶ Email us for more information at: lpm@abanet.org
▶ Check us out on the Internet: http://www.abanet.org/lpm

750 N. LAKE SHORE DRIVE
CHICAGO, IL 60611
PHONE: (312) 988-5619
FAX: (312) 988-5820
Email: lpm@abanet.org

*I understand that Section dues include a $24 basic subscription to Law Practice Management; this subscription charge is not deductible from the dues and additional subscriptions are not available at this rate. Membership dues in the American Bar Association are not deductible as charitable contributions for income tax purposes. However, such dues may be deductible as a business expense.*